*Just Imagine* Stan

# DC UNIVERSE

BOOK
1

STAN LEE

Writer

JOE KUBERT
JIM LEE
JOHN BUSCEMA
DAVE GIBBONS

Artists

AND MANY MORE OF THE FINEST TALENTS IN COMICS...

"JUST IMAGINE STAN LEE CREATING THE DC UNIVERSE" initiated by

MICHAEL USLAN

JUST IMAGINE STAN LEE CREATING THE DC UNIVERSE: BOOK ONE



DC Comics, 1700 Broadway, New York, NY 10019
A division of Warner Bros. – An AOL Time Warner Company
Printed in Canada. First Printing.
ISBN: 1-56389-891-8
Cover illustration by Stuart Immonen.

contents

# Introduction

by Michael Uslan

Once upon a time, on a warm L.A. night in June 1989 at the world premiere of the motion picture Batman, hundreds of swankily swathed V.I.P.s swarmed its stars and swooned over them. Me? I might have been the Executive Producer of the movie, but I was a comic book fanboy at heart, and I raced over to the two biggest stars I could see while looking through my four-color glasses: Bob Kane, creator of Batman, and Stan Lee, co-creator of almost everything else in comic book history. As I joined them by the little hot dog hors d'oeuvres, Stan and Bob were busy teasing each other:

Bob: "If I had originally drawn your Spider-Man, I could have made it successful for you, Stan!"

Stan: "And if I had written Batman, Bob, it would've been so totally different that —"

I never heard the rest of that sentence because my mind was already trying to conceive what a Stan Lee Batman might have been.

That night, a dream I had to produce a dark, serious movie version of Batman came true. Another dream I had about one day working creatively with my idol, Stan "The Man" Lee, took root that same night. It had taken me fourteen years to achieve that first dream. It would take twelve more to achieve the second.

FADE OUT
FADE IN

It's June 1999. I meet Stan for lunch in L.A. Borrowing a phrase from DC Comics' classic ad for the first appearance of The Justice League of America, ("Just Imagine! Your favorite super-heroes together in one comic magazine!"), I said to Smilin' Stan, "Just imagine if you had been at DC instead of Marvel from the beginning. How would you in your own unique style have created DC's characters Superman, Batman, Wonder Woman, and the JLA?"

When I suggested this could really happen, Stan was intrigued and excited by the idea. He saw it as an opportunity to pay tribute to the creators of these masterpieces of pop culture in a creative exercise that would permit him to work with the greatest artists in the history of comicbookdom. Stan had but one caveat and one question first. The caveat was that this series not be considered some misguided attempt to "fix" or "improve" these super-heroes, which needed no fixing or improving. There was no disagreement on my part. Then I asked him what his question was. Stan replied, "Are you nuts?!" He thought DC Comics would never go for such a wild idea. Not in a million years!

FADE OUT
FADE IN

A million years later (actually, it was a week), I was back in New York asking Paul Levitz at DC what he thought of the idea. He had one caveat and one question. The caveat was that it be an even bigger project — a year-long series instead of just four books — due to its historical importance. And his one question to me? "Can you just imagine how much fun this will be?"

There could be no great project without a great editor. Clearly, this was a job for... Mike Carlin, super DC Executive Editor! It was at a classic Hollywood power lunch you hear tell about (in Stan's L.A. office) that the names of the first artists to contact about the new project took the form of an official list — penned on a napkin. Unbelievable? Yes. True? Yes.

What "We Are the World" was to the music business, "Stan Lee's Just Imagine" became to the world of comic books — a collection of the best artists in the business. As a result, within this very tome will be found the magnificent artwork of the legendary Joe Kubert, who co-creates Stan's BATMAN. Multiple generations of fans hail Kubert's work since the 1940s on Tarzan, Hawkman, Sgt. Rock, Tor, and countless other features. Rounding out the Batman issue is the artistry of Michael Kaluta, who not only redefined The Shadow for a new generation of comic book readers, but presented the world with one of the sleekest, most romanticized versions of Batman ever to see print.

DC HOUSE AD, CIRCA 1960

It's Jim Lee who co-creates WONDER WOMAN with Stan. Jim's artistry on *X-Men* put him on the map, and his work since then for Marvel, Image, WildStorm, and, coming soon, DC's BATMAN, continues to grow the legend. Joining Jim on the Wonder Woman book is fan favorite Gene Colan. With Stan Lee in the days of the Marvel

Bullpen, Gene, with inker Tom Palmer, created some of the most famous artistic interpretations the world had ever seen of Dr. Strange, Daredevil, Iron Man, and Sub-Mariner.

It was a historic event to witness Stan Lee and the great John Buscema reunite for a re-imagining of DC's SUPERMAN. Buscema's artwork on Stan's Silver Surfer book has been critically acclaimed as some of the finest art ever to appear in comic books. Buscema's other work on The Avengers and Conan the Barbarian served to cement his reputation as one of the greatest of the greats. His art within these pages represents some of his last published work before his untimely passing this year. Also on board the Superman book is cartoonist Kyle Baker, whose cutting-edge designs and mastery of humor brings to life Joe, Midge, and the entire sleazy gang at Fly-By-Night Comics Group.

Dave Gibbons revolutionized the world of comics with his imaginative, expressive, and powerful artwork on the famous WATCHMEN graphic novel that he co-created with the great Alan Moore. His interpretation of Stan Lee's GREEN LANTERN becomes a key, defining book in the building storyline of the "Just Imagine" series. José Luis Garciá-López, with inker Josef Rubinstein, the artist who brought new life to the image of Superman in the '70s and '80s, rounds out the Green Lantern book as he explores the impact of human heroes in a world where super-heroes are the ones who capture the limelight.

Once Mike Carlin made sure that Stan had the best artists for each book, he turned to the line-up. Working with Stan in the selection process, he offered a menu of DC super-heroes and super-groups that read like a Who's Who of comic books. Stan's final choices of Batman, Wonder Woman, Superman, Green Lantern, Flash, the JLA, Robin, Shazam, Aquaman, Catwoman, Sandman, and the Crisis left for another day such possibilities as the Teen Titans, the Legion of Super-Heroes, Green Arrow, Plastic Man, Martian Manhunter, and more. For now, Stan could bring the stylistic touch of his approach to Thor to Wonder Woman, the Human Torch to Aquaman, Silver Surfer to Green Lantern, Spider-Man to Catwoman, the Hulk and his 1950s monsters like Fin Fang Foom to Shazam, Dr. Strange to Sandman, and the cosmic characters and noble villains in the tradition of Eternity, Galactus, Dr. Doom, and Nightmare to the Crisis.

## CUT TO

There's much, much more to what Stan Lee brings to a comic book than merely a stylistic touch. After all, the man revolutionized the comic book world beginning in 1961 in a way that enabled his readership (which quickly broke through traditional comic book demographics to reach the university crowd and beyond) to be able to suspend its disbelief easily and buy into characters and situations that, while fantastic, felt real. He began by setting his tales of super-heroics within actual cities. Names like Metropolis and Gotham City were replaced by New York, Flushing, and Westchester. Not only were the places real — it felt like Stan's characters and even the general population in the background of his stories were real, too. Before Stan, if a super-hero was portrayed battling a monster in the middle of some mythical city, the man-in-the-street in each panel would react, "Aaaah! It's a monster! Run!" But when Stan wrote his stories, he got into the heads of real New Yorkers, and the reactions of his passersby were more like, "Hey, lookit the monster, Gladys! Dino must be back in town shooting another King Kong sequel!"

When it was time for Stan to craft his major characters, he made them as colorful as any in the history of comics, but he also made them textured and conflicted — something the medium had never experienced before. Heroes were arguing with each other. Lovers suffered from the emotional stress of relationships in crisis. Heroes were in conflict with the very public they wanted so much to help — a public wary of any bizarrely behaving person clad in a mask and tights who claimed to be a good vigilante looking out for their best interests. All these conflicts paled in comparison to the self-doubts, the soul-searching, the inner torments each Stan Lee hero tended to experience. Stan's hero, unlike all the super-heroes in comics before, often perceived his special powers as a curse rather than as a boon.

Superman, Batman, and most of the comic book heroes that came before Stan had many great qualities, but a sense of humor was rarely one of them. In Stan's approach, there was humor in the dialogue of the heroes ("I'm your friendly neighborhood Spider-Man, available for weddings, bar mitzvahs, and other catered affairs!"), in the reaction of commonplace people to the heroes ("Seeing Thor's hair reminds me I have to make a beauty parlor appointment this week!"), and in the personalities of supporting characters (Willy Lumpkin, the Fantastic Four's mailman, attempted to join the super-group based on his ability to wiggle his ears real good). Even desperate situations involved humor in a Stan story, as when in the middle of a huge crisis, Reed Richards was tied up on a phone call to the F.F. hotline from a lady who dialed the wrong number and was relentlessly trying to order a pizza to be delivered to her apartment.

No one in comics had ever written dialogue that rang so real, so true. No other writer in comics imbued his characters with such clearly defined, though complex, personalities. Some of his heroes could spew philosophy and bring a touch of Shakespeare to the comics. Some of his villains were given a sense of nobility and presented in shades of gray so it was not always clear how harshly they should be judged.

Stan may have entertained his readers as they were never entertained by comics before, but he also made them think. Themes of alienation and acceptance were the undercurrent of every hit comics character, from Spider-Man to the Hulk. Stan's most famous theme, succinctly summing up the point of the entire super-hero genre, was profound: "With great power comes great responsibility." Stan's themes were always important and always struck a chord with his growing audience. He made his audience care — care about the characters and about the super soap operas that constituted their lives.

Stan was always a wizard of communication with his readers. No editor of any comic book company ever had what felt like a personal dialogue with his caring audience the way Stan did. He never wrote down to them, and never was afraid to admit mistakes he may have made on rare occasions. Readers always knew he was in touch, had a handle on contemporary stories that were always smart, clever, fun, as well as very cool and hip, often presented with the feel of a contemporary mythology. In Stan's universe, characters could die without "coming back" time after time, super-heroes might not rely on traditional super-costumes, and major changes could happen at any time to any major, starring character. The rules had indeed changed.

And, of course, if Stan was creating characters, you could count on most of them having alliterative names (Reed Richards, Bruce Banner, Sue Storm, Peter Parker, Matt Murdoch, Scott Summers, Warren Worthington, Wyatt Wingfoot, etc.).

So then, just imagine if Stan Lee had begun his career at DC Comics instead of Marvel. Just imagine if that circumstance led to an entire new universe of comic book heroes and villains, a new mythology known as DC Comics' "Staniverse." The possibilities are endless — and awesome. What cosmic event could precipitate a banding together of all of Stan Lee's newly created JLA? Wouldn't Stan have to create the comic book industry's most powerful, original super-villain to face off with them? Yes, he would! And so he has...

Books 1-4: Meet Stan Lee's Batman, Wonder Woman, Superman, and Green Lantern. The Staniverse — and comic book history — begins now with a Big Bang and starts us on the road to CRISIS, perhaps Stan Lee's most cosmic saga of all!

It matters not if you started reading comic books in the Golden Age, the Silver Age, or last Wednesday, and it matters not if you're a DC Fan-Addict or like to Make Mine Marvel — JUST IMAGINE STAN LEE brings you the best of both worlds in the form of a newly created one.

They said that before Stan Lee would ever write for DC Comics, Henry Ford would build a car for GM, the President of Coca-Cola would take the Pepsi Challenge and choose Pepsi, and the Yankees and Mets would meet in a Subway Series. Well, one out of three ain't bad!

DISSOLVE

**— Michael Uslan**
**2002**

JOE KUBERT
01

THE NIGHT IS DARK AND STAR-LESS...
...THE POUNDING RAIN IS COLD.
BUT THE HEART OF WAYNE WILLIAMS IS COLDER STILL...
...FOR IT BEATS WITH A SILENT, SEETHING RAGE.
THEY GUNNED HIM DOWN.
HE NEVER HAD A CHANCE.
HE WAS A COP. HE DID HIS DUTY.
YEAH... AND THAT'S THE THANKS HE GOT.
HE WOULDN'T HAVE WANTED US TO BE BITTER, BOY.
I CAN'T HELP IT, MA... I'M HURTIN'.
JOE KUBERT

HE SPENT HIS LIFE TRYIN' TO MAKE A DIFFERENCE...
...AND WHERE DID IT GET 'IM?
THIS AIN'T A NEIGHBORHOOD --IT'S A WAR ZONE.

STOP IT! YOU'RE HURTING HIM!
YEAH, RIGHT! THAT'S THE IDEA!

YOU GOT A PROBLEM WITH THAT, LADY?

C'MON, MA... W-WE GOTTA GO! IT AIN'T OUR FIGHT.
THE GUY PROBABLY DESERVED WHAT HE WAS GETTIN'.

HEY, HANDZ... WASN'T THAT SAM WILLIAMS' KID?
YEAH... THEY JUST BURIED HIS OLD MAN.
ONE LESS CREEP FOR US T' WORRY ABOUT.

HOW COULD YOU SAY THAT POOR BOY DESERVED TO BE BEATEN?
I HADDA SAY SOMETHIN', MOM... TO GET YOU AWAY.
YOU DON'T KNOW WHO YOU WERE MESSIN' WITH.

SLEEP DOESN'T ALWAYS COME EASY IN THE INNER CITY... BUT FINALLY...
CAN'T BE LATE FOR WORK THIS MORNING.
MA WILL NEED MY PAY MORE THAN EVER NOW.
I WAS ALL SET T' QUIT TODAY... BUT WITH DAD GONE, I CAN'T.
NOW I GOTTA PUT UP WITH THAT CRUDDY BOSS OF MINE.
SUPER MINI
MOVE IT, WILLIAMS. I PAY YA TO STACK THOSE CANS... NOT PLAY WITH 'EM.
YEAH, SURE... OKAY, OKAY!
SUPER MINI
THERE'S HANDZ.
YA DON'T CATCH HIM WORKIN' IN A NOWHERE DUMP LIKE THIS.
HE MAY BE JUST A HOOD... BUT HE SURE LIVES THE BIG LIFE.
ANY GUY WHO COULD RATE A FOXY CHICK LIKE THAT...!
LISTEN! DO YOU HEAR A CAR GUNNING ITS ENGINE?
YEAH... SO WHAT? SOME DUDE JUMPIN' A LIGHT IS ALL.
NO! IT'S HEADIN' FOR US!
SALE

THERE HE IS! NOW'S OUR CHANCE!
BRRRP POW POW
HE AIN'T CRASHIN' OUR TURF NO MORE!
RRRP
THEY'RE AFTER ME!
MINI MARKE
SALE
SKRREEEEEEEEEE
HANDZ--!
SPANG
CRACK
BWEEEE
GOTTA DUCK BEHIND THIS CAR!
THE GIRL'S IN THE LINE OF FIRE!
DOESN'T KNOW WHAT T' DO!
SHE'S JUST STANDIN' THERE...
...FROZEN WITH FEAR!
GET DOWN!
'FORE YA CATCH A SLUG!
CRACK CRACK CRAK

TAKE OFF!
HE GOT THE MESSAGE!
N MARKET

HEY! WHO SAID YOU COULD MESS WITH MY LADY?
NO TWO-BIT PUNK ACTS LIKE A HERO WHEN I'M AROUND!
I--JUST TRIED T'HELP...

YEAH? TRY THAT AGAIN AN' YA'LL GET WHAT YER FATHER GOT!

NOW... GIT LOST, LOSER!

N-NO ONE TALKS ABOUT MY FATHER LIKE TH--
¡UMPHH!
SLAP

CAN'T SAY I DIDN'T WARN YA!
YOU GOT A DEATH WISH? I'LL TRY'N OBLIGE.

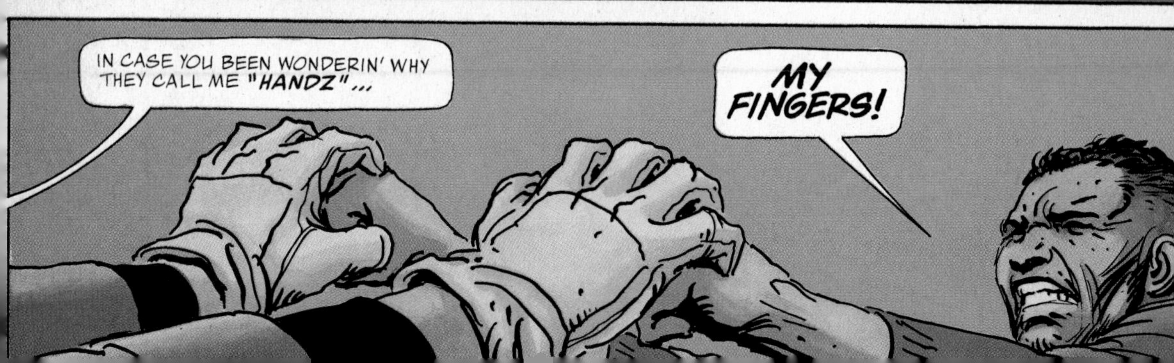
IN CASE YOU BEEN WONDERIN' WHY THEY CALL ME "HANDZ"...
MY FINGERS!

I NOTICE YOU AIN'T TELLIN' ME **WHO** I CAN TALK ABOUT... **NOW!**

I NOTICE YOU AIN'T SAYIN' **ANYTHING,** RIGHT?

**OWW!**

L-LOOK, I DIDN'T MEAN--

DID I **ASK** YA WHAT YA MEANT?

DO I **CARE** WHAT YA MEANT? I'LL GIVE YA **THREE GUESSES...**

N-NO... LET HIM GO... P-PLEASE!
SURE, BABY. SOON AS I GIVE HIM SOMETHIN' TO REMEMBER ME BY!
HANDZ NO FEET
I'M DOIN' 'IM A FAVOR.
IF I FIX IT SO HE CAN'T NEVER MAKE A FIST...
...HE'LL STAY OUTTA FIGHTS AND HE WON'T GIT HURT.
LET HIM GO NOW... OR WE'RE THROUGH!
AWRIGHT... AWRIGHT. THE PUNK AIN'T WORTH THE TROUBLE.
DON'T MAKE ANY FUTURE PLANS, KNOW WHAT I MEAN?
YOU AIN'T SEEN THE LAST OF ME.
H-HE COULDA CRUSHED MY FINGERS... LIKE PAPER...
HANDZ NO FEET
DAD'S GONE. I'VE BEEN THREATENED BY HANDZ.
THINGS CAN'T GET ANY WORSE.
THE NEXT DAY PROVES THAT WAYNE IS A BAD PROPHET...
FREEZE!
DON'T NOBODY MOVE!
CREAM
TRY OUR N
SODA
I KNOW THAT VOICE!

WE GOT HERE AS SOON AS WE COULD, WAYNE.
YEAH! THANKS FOR THE **TIP,** MAN!
WE **KNEW** WE COULD COUNT ON YA, WAYNE.
WH-WHAT ARE YOU **TALKIN'** ABOUT?
**YOU SLIMY FINK!** YOU SET ME UP!

LATER...
LUCKY HE WAS ONLY HIT IN THE SHOULDER!
YEAH... BUT WHO WAS IT SLUGGED THE PERP?
STILL LATER...
THAT WILLIAMS KID WAS ONE O' THEM!
UNGRATE-FUL PUNK... AFTER ME GIVIN' 'IM A JOB!
THEY MUSTA BEEN FIGHTIN' OVER THE MONEY AFTER I GOT SHOT.
THAT'S HOW HE GOT KNOCKED OUT.
YOU'VE BEEN FOUND GUILTY OF ARMED ROBBERY...
I-- I DIDN'T DO IT, MOM. I SWEAR...
I'LL PRAY FOR YOU, SON.
LET'S GO.
AS THE SAYING GOES, JUSTICE IS BLIND.
SOMETIMES--TOO BLIND.
IT WAS HANDZ.
HE FRAMED ME... PUT THAT GUN IN MY HAND.
BUT I'LL GET EVEN.
NO MATTER HOW LONG IT TAKES...
I'LL FIND A WAY TO PAY HIM BACK!

IN THE WEEKS THAT FOLLOW...
JUST MY CRUMMY LUCK TO HAVE TO WORK AT A DUMB **SEWING MACHINE.**
WHATCHA DOIN', WILLIAMS? SEWIN' A **DRESS** FER YER **PROM?**
**NO WAY** YOU WUZ BUSTED FER ARMED ROBBERY...
**I'M** BETTIN' THEY GOTCHA FER WEARIN' THE **WRONG MAKEUP.**

HEY, LOOK AT THE BRIGHT SIDE...
HE'LL MAKE SOMEONE A REAL NICE **WIFE.**

MOVE ALONG... LEAVE THE KID ALONE.
DON'T WORRY. WE DON'T WANT **NO PART** OF 'IM.

I JUST GOTTA TAKE IT ONE DAY AT A TIME.
IF I STOP T' FEEL **SORRY** FOR MY-SELF, I'LL **NEVER** MAKE IT OUTTA HERE!

HAVE TO GET MY MIND OFF HANDZ... OR I'LL END UP IN A **PADDED CELL.**
MUST THINK OF SOMETHING **ELSE. ANYTHING.**
MAYBE COUNT THE **BATS** THAT FLY BY AT NIGHT.

JUST A BUNCHA UGLY NIGHT-FLYERS. EVERYONE HATES 'EM.
REMINDS ME OF **ME.**

I'LL BET THEY'RE HUNGRY.

I WAS RIGHT ABOUT **THAT** ONE.
LOOK AT 'IM GRABBIN' THOSE CRUMBS.

C'MON IN, LITTLE GUY... I CAN USE THE COMPANY.

EITHER HE TRUSTS ME... OR HE'S TOO HUNGRY TO CARE.

UGLY AS HE IS... HE KINDA **GROWS** ON YA.

TAKE YOUR TIME, LITTLE GUY.
I FIGURE THE **LONGER** I STAY HERE... THE BETTER YOU'LL LOOK TO ME.

WEEKS TURN INTO MONTHS, BUT THE ROUTINE NEVER VARIES...
YOU'RE GETTIN' TO KNOW ME, AREN'TCHA, LITTLE GUY?
YOU'RE THE BEST FRIEND I'VE GOT.
YOU'RE THE ONLY FRIEND I'VE GOT... THAT'S FOR SURE.
ELSEWHERE...
I TOLDJA WE'D HAVE IT MADE ONCE WE SMASHED THE HORZOCK GANG.
YEAH, HANDZ... CAN'T NO ONE STOP US NOW!
EVERYONE KNOWS YOU'RE KING OF THE 'HOOD.
GLASS
FERGET THE 'HOOD. THAT'S SMALL TIME STUFF.
I'M JUST GETTIN' STARTED.
WE'RE GONNA TAKE OVER EVERY GANG IN THE CITY.
WHAT'S WITH YOU, NITA? WHY THE SOUR FACE?
I- I JUST CAN'T FORGET THAT POOR BOY YOU FRAMED MONTHS AGO.
HE'S STILL IN JAIL. ISN'T THERE SOME-THING YOU CAN--
SHUDDUP! HE GOT WHAT HE DESERVED!
DON'T EVER MENTION 'IM AGAIN... HEAR?

EVERYONE'S PUMPIN' IRON. MAYBE *I* OUGHTA TRY IT.
IF I DIDN'T HAVE TO SPEND SO MUCH TIME WITH THAT CRUMMY **SEWING MACHINE**.
WAY T'GO, **KORGO**.
THIS IS GETTIN' **BORIN'**.
I NEED SOMETHIN' **ELSE** TO LIFT.
WELL, WHADDAYA KNOW... **JUST** WHAT I'M LOOKIN' FOR.
C'MERE, OLD MAN.
IF YOU AIN'T A **LIFTER**...
...THAT MAKES YOU A **LIFTEE**.
YOU KNOW THE RULES... **EVERYONE'S** GOT TO EXERCISE...
SO... I'M JUST GONNA **HELP** YA OUT.
TAKE A DEEP BREATH... THE AIR'S **FRESHER** UP THERE.

C'MON, KORGO, L-LEAVE 'IM ALONE. HE WASN'T BOTHERIN' YOU...

YEAH, PUNK, YER **RIGHT**.

HE **WUZN'T** BOTHERIN' ME...

...BUT **YOU ARE**.

AND KORGO **DON' LIKE** BEIN' BOTHERED.

CRACK

WE BETTER SPLIT, KORGO... BEFORE THE GUARDS COME.
RELAX. AIN'T NO RULE AGAINST GETTIN' SOME EXERCISE.

Y-YOU SHOULDN'T HAVE INTERFERED, SON.
YEAH... I KINDA... REALIZE THAT... NOW.

THAT'S MY PROBLEM, I GUESS... I SHOOT OFF MY MOUTH WITHOUT THINKIN'.
A GOOD IMPULSE IS OFTEN A SIGN OF A GOOD SPIRIT.

YOU'RE YOUNG AND HEALTHY... YOU'VE GOT GOOD POTENTIAL.
NO NEED TO BE A VICTIM.

IT'S TOO LATE FOR ME... BUT THOSE BAR-BELLS... USE THEM.
BUILD YOUR-SELF UP.

THERE'S A LIBRARY. DEVELOP YOUR MIND, TOO.
DON'T LET YOUR TIME HERE GO TO WASTE.

DON'T TRY TO BECOME SCHWARZEN-EGGER OVERNIGHT.
START SLOW. IT'S THE REPS THAT DO IT.
I... DON'T CARE... HOW HARD IT IS... OR... HOW LONG IT TAKES...
RIGHT! WE GOT NOTHIN' BUT TIME.

NO PRISONER EVER WORKED HARDER AT BODY-BUILDING THAN WAYNE WILLIAMS.
NO PRISONER WAS MORE DETERMINED TO BECOME THE BEST HE COULD BE THAN WAYNE WILLIAMS.
NO PRISONER GAINED MUSCLE MASS FASTER OR MORE POWERFULLY THAN WAYNE WILLIAMS.
NO PRISONER WAS AS FILLED WITH A BURNING DESIRE FOR VENGEANCE AS WAYNE WILLIAMS.
IT ACTUALLY TOOK WAYNE MANY *MONTHS* TO BE-COME A POWERHOUSE.
BUT SINCE WE'VE GOT A LOT MORE STORY TO TELL, WE'LL TAKE LITERARY LICENSE AND CUT THAT SEQUENCE SHORT...
BETWEEN WEIGHTS AND SEWING MACHINES, WAYNE BONDS WITH HIS ADJACENT CELL MATE...
WHAT KIND OF A SCIENTIST WERE YOU?
ACTUALLY, I'M A DOCTOR OF *PHYSICS*. BUT I'M AN *INVENTOR* AT HEART.
HE SAID HE HOLDS MORE THAN A DOZEN PATENTS.
A GREAT GUY LIKE HIM DOESN'T BELONG *HERE*.
FINALLY...
I'M GETTING OUT TOMORROW, WAYNE.
I'LL GIVE YOU MY ADDRESS. KEEP IN TOUCH.
I'LL MISS YA, MAN.

FROM THE OUTSIDE IT SEEMS NO DIFFERENT THAN THE COUNTLESS OTHER CHURCHES THAT DOT LOS ANGELES...

...BUT... LOOKS CAN BE DECEIVING!

Church of Eternal Empowerment
REVEREND DOMINIC DARRK

OUR CHURCH MUST GROW.

OUR POWER MUST IN-CREASE.

OUR MISSION MUST NOT FAIL!

WE MUST BRING THE BLESSING OF ETERNAL EMPOWERMENT TO ALL MANKIND.

TO DO SO REQUIRES MORE DISCIPLES.

...AS THREE FULL TIERS OF IRON CELL DOORS SWING SLOWLY OPEN...

H-HEY! WHAT'S HAPPENIN'?

I DUNNO. BUT I AIN'T COMPLAININ'.

SOMETHIN' MUST'A JAMMED THE AUTOMATIC LOCK-UP CIRCUIT.

THEN... WHAT ARE WE WAITIN' ON?

NOW'S OUR CHANCE TO GET OUTTA HERE!

WAIT! USE YOUR HEADS!
YOU'LL NEVER MAKE IT PAST THE GUARD STATIONS.
SHUDDUP, MAN! THIS IS OUR BIG CHANCE--AN' WE AIN'T BLOWIN' IT!
BUT THE BULLS HAVE GUNS! WE GOT NO HARDWARE.
DON'T NEED NONE. ALL WE GOTTA DO IS GRAB THE WARDEN.

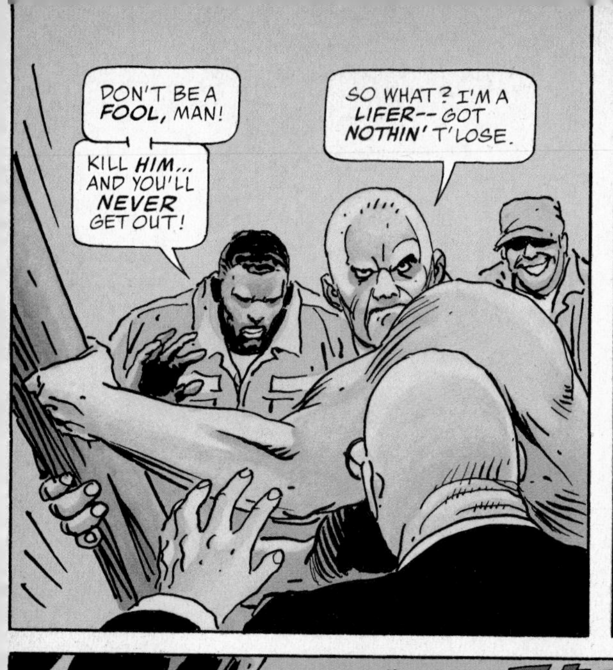
DON'T BE A FOOL, MAN!
KILL HIM... AND YOU'LL NEVER GET OUT!
SO WHAT? I'M A LIFER-- GOT NOTHIN' T'LOSE.

TOO BAD, WARDEN-- I'M OUTTA PATIENCE--
--AND YOU'RE OUTTA TIME!

THUMP
NO!

YOU CAN'T KILL SOMEONE FOR DOIN' HIS JOB!
YER A DEAD MAN, HEAR?
WE'LL TEAR YA APART!
MPFFF

GIVE IT YOUR BEST SHOT!
I DON'T TEAR THAT EASY...

YOU DIRTY WARDEN LOVER...
HOLD 'IM! I WANNA FINISH 'IM OFF MY-SELF!
WANT ME, CREEP? COME 'N' GET ME!
GOT NEWS FOR YA...
YOU SHOULD'A STAYED IN YOUR CELLS!
WHY... WHY'D YA DO IT? WHY'D YA STOP OUR ESCAPE?
YOU'LL NEVER KNOW.

ONE WEEK LATER...
I'M LOSIN' PATIENCE, NITA... I AIN'T GONNA WAIT FOREVER.
I'M SORRY, HANDZ. I-I'M STILL NOT READY FOR MARRIAGE.
YOU AIN'T NEVER GONNA DO BETTER'N ME, GIRL. I GOT MONEY, POWER AND--
HEY... LOOKA THIS!
REMEMBER THAT WIMP WAYNE WILLIAMS? HE'S IN THE PAPER!
DAILY CLARION
HE'S GETTIN' OUTTA THE SLAMMER--GOT HIMSELF A PARDON.
WARDEN WITH WAYNE WILLIAMS
MAYBE THEY LEARNED HE WAS INNOCENT...
NO WAY! THE RAT JUST TURNED AGAINST THE OTHER CONS.
HE'S THE ONLY ONE WHO CAN FINGER US!
THE PAPER SAYS HE'S A HERO...
SHUDDUP! HE'S NOTHIN', Y'UNDERSTAND?
WE'RE GONNA FIND 'IM... AN' FINISH 'IM... FOR GOOD!

I NEED A PLACE TO STAY. GOTTA THINK... AND PLAN.
THIS'LL HAVE TO DO.
HOTEL
VAN

YOU GOT EX-CON WRITTEN ALL OVER YA!
FIVE BUCKS A NIGHT... PAY IN ADVANCE OR GIT LOST.
I HEAR YA, SLIME-BALL.

HANDZ MUSTA READ THAT I BEEN PARDONED.
HE WON'T LIKE ME RUNNIN' LOOSE... KNOWIN' WHAT I KNOW. SO... I'LL LET 'IM STEW IN HIS OWN JUICE FOR AWHILE.

HE'S BECOME THE GANGS' HEAD HONCHO. GOT A TON O' MONEY AND HIRED GUNS.
PROBABLY GOT A HIT OUT FOR ME ALREADY.

SO... YOU'N ME ARE GONNA KEEP A LOW PROFILE, OKAY?

YOU AIN'T MUCH... BUT... YOU'RE THE ONLY FRIEND I GOT.

FIRST OFF, I GOTTA MAKE SURE I AIN'T A SITTIN' DUCK FOR HANDZ'S TRIGGER MEN.

THE HARDER IT IS TO FIND ME... THE MORE UP-TIGHT HE'LL GET.
AND THAT'S HOW I WANT IT.

HOPE YOU DIDN'T JUST LIKE ME FOR MY PRETTY FACE, LITTLE GUY.

BUT I DON'T FIGURE LOOKS MEAN ALL THAT MUCH... TO A BAT.
HOTE

THE IMPORTANT THING IS... HANDZ MUSN'T FIND ME.
NOT TILL I FIGURE OUT THE BEST WAY TO BRING 'IM DOWN.

FINISHED.

THAT WAS EASY. NOW COMES THE HARD PART.

HANDZ IS POWERFUL... WELL-PROTECTED. PROBABLY THINKS I'M JUST A PUNK, NO THREAT TO 'IM.
SO I NEED JUST ONE MORE THING... MONEY!... TO LEVEL THE PLAYING FIELD.
LET'S SEE IF THIS CRUMMY TV WORKS.

A WRESTLING RING.

WHAT A PHONEY CROCK...!

I COULD MAKE A BETTER COSTUME IN MY SLEEP...

...BUT... THE FANS EAT IT UP!

GOTTA ADMIT... THEY'RE FUN TO WATCH.

AS CORNY AS THEY ARE...

...THEY SURE PUT ON A GREAT SHOW.

AND ACCORDIN' TO THE ANNOUNCER, MOST OF 'EM MAKE A PILE O' DOUGH.

THERE'S MY ANSWER! STARIN' ME RIGHT IN THE FACE! ALL I GOTTA DO IS BUY SOME FABRIC.

WAIT UP, LITTLE GUY... I'LL BE RIGHT BACK!

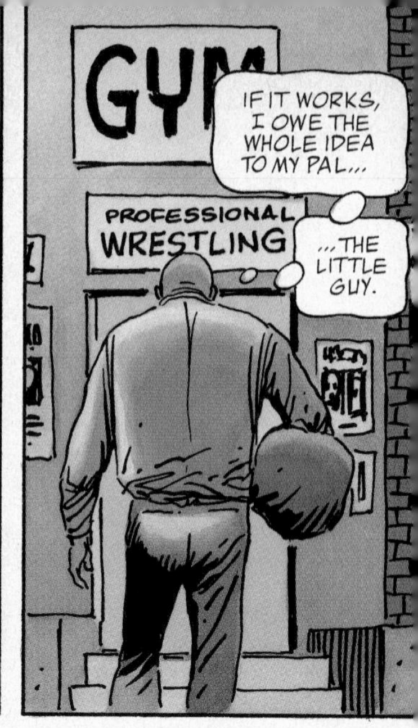


CHAMPIONSHIP WRESTLING
BOUTS
MADIS
HEY! YOU GOT YOURSELF A NEW WRESTLER!
HUH? WHO'RE YOU?
YOU CAN CALL ME-- BATMAN!

BATMAN, SHMATMAN. IT TAKES MORE THAN A COSTUME, MISTER...
LET'S SEE HOW LONG YA CAN LAST IN THE RING WITH STEAMROLLER.
I GIVE THAT CORNBALL 10 SECONDS.
TEN SECONDS, HUH?
THAT'S MORE THAN I NEED.
STEAMROLLERS MAY BE BIG'N STRONG-- BUT, IN CASE YOU HAVEN'T HEARD...
...THEY'RE TOO FREAKIN' SLOW!
DIDJA SEE THAT?
NOBODY EVER DONE THAT TO STEAMROLLER.
HE MADE IT LOOK EASY!
WHO IS HE?
I DON'T CARE WHO HE IS... SIGN 'IM UP-- NOW!

AND SO IT BEGINS...
AFTER PRISON, THIS IS A PICNIC!
I'M STRONGER AND FASTER THAN MOST OF 'EM...
AND THERE'S SOMETHIN' ELSE GOIN' FOR ME...
...EVERYONE'S SCARED OF BATS!
SO MY COSTUME THROWS 'EM OFF.
THE MORE I WIN... THE MORE THEY PAY ME!
SO AIN'T NO WAY BATMAN'S GONNA LOSE!
WITHIN A FEW SHORT WEEKS, BATMAN HAS BE-COME THE BIGGEST NAME IN WRESTLING...
...AND STILL NO ONE KNOWS HIS REAL IDENTITY.
AND AS LONG AS I NEVER UNMASK IN PUBLIC... THEY'LL KEEP COMIN', HOPIN' SOMEONE'LL TEAR OFF MY MASK.

BEFORE LONG, THE MEDIA HAVE A FEEDING FRENZY OVER THE MYSTERIOUS **BATMAN**...

...ENDLESS TV INTERVIEWS...

***WHY*** DO YOU REFUSE TO LET THE PUBLIC KNOW WHAT YOU ***REALLY LOOK LIKE?***

HOW D'YOU KNOW THIS ***ISN'T*** MY REAL FACE?

IT'S TIME TO GO AFTER HANDZ!
I'LL GET ONLY ONE SHOT AT HIM... AND IF I FAIL ...IT'S OVER!
THE PLACE HE LIVES IN IS LIKE AN IMPREGNABLE FORTRESS. HE'S GOT ARMED BODYGUARDS AROUND THE CLOCK. HIS HANDS ARE LETHAL WEAPONS. THEY SAY HE FEARS NOTHING.
BUT... HE'S NEVER FACED BATMAN BEFORE!
HOLLYWOO

NOW THAT I'VE GOT EVERYTHING MONEY CAN BUY... THERE'S STILL **ONE DECISION** I HAVE TO MAKE.

IF I'M LUCKY ENOUGH TO DEFEAT **HANDZ**... WHAT **THEN?**

REPUTED BOSS LEADER **HANDZ HORGUM** FLAUNTS HIS POWER...

...APPARENTLY UNTOUCHABLE BY THE LAW...

...WHILE RECENTLY RELEASED **DOCTOR GRANT** IS HAVING A HARD TIME...

WHAT COMES **NEXT?**

WHAT DO I DO WITH THE **REST** OF MY LIFE?

I'M IN LUCK... THERE HE IS!
WHO--?

DO YOU KNOW WHO I AM?
OF COURSE. BATMAN... THE WRESTLER. YOU'VE BEEN ALL OVER THE MEDIA.
WHAT'RE YOU DOING IN A DUMP LIKE THIS?
EX-CONS DON'T USUALLY GET HIGH-PAYING JOBS.

YEAH ... WELL, NOW ONE OF 'EM WILL!
YOU-- YOU'RE WAYNE! WAYNE WILLIAMS! BUT HOW--?

IT'S A LONG STORY... I NEED YOUR HELP.
IT'S BEEN A LONG TIME SINCE I'VE HEARD THAT... FROM ANYONE.

YOU'RE THE ONLY ONE I TRUST.
THE ONLY ONE WHO'LL EVER KNOW THAT BATMAN IS WAYNE WILLIAMS.

I HAVE MONEY... SKILL... AND STRENGTH. BUT YOU HAVE WISDOM AND KNOWLEDGE.

I WANT THAT WISDOM, THAT KNOWLEDGE. I'LL PAY YOU... TO BE MY PARTNER.
BUT-- WHAT IS IT YOU WANT ME TO DO?
COME WITH ME.

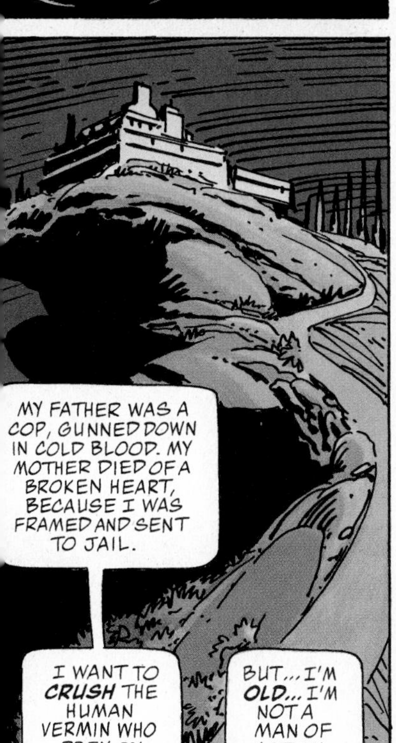
MY FATHER WAS A COP, GUNNED DOWN IN COLD BLOOD. MY MOTHER DIED OF A BROKEN HEART, BECAUSE I WAS FRAMED AND SENT TO JAIL.

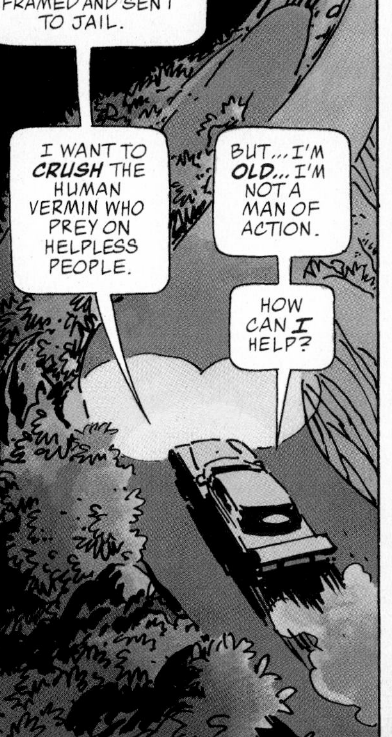
I WANT TO CRUSH THE HUMAN VERMIN WHO PREY ON HELPLESS PEOPLE.
BUT... I'M OLD... I'M NOT A MAN OF ACTION.
HOW CAN I HELP?

I'VE TOLD YOU. IT'S YOUR BRAIN I WANT. WE'LL MAKE A PERFECT TEAM.
I'VE GOT IT ALL FIGURED OUT...

DO YOU REMEMBER TELLING ME TO STUDY THE BAT? YOU SAID BATS HAVE SOME POWERS BETTER THAN HUMANS.
YES... THAT'S TRUE.

HERE, I FITTED OUT A LAB FOR YOU.
I WANT YOU TO DUPLICATE THOSE BAT POWERS FOR ME... ANY WAY YOU CAN.

BATS SEE BEST IN THE DARK.
"I CAN ADD BUILT-IN NIGHT VISION LENSES TO YOUR MASK."

BATS HEAR THROUGH A SORT OF RADAR SENSE.
"IT WOULDN'T BE HARD TO GIVE YOUR MASK AN ELECTRONIC SENSOR THAT WILL MAGNIFY SOUND."

IF A BAT CAN FLY, WHY NOT YOU?
"YOUR CAPE COULD BE CONFIGURED LIKE BAT WINGS... SO YOU CAN GLIDE ON CURRENTS OF AIR."

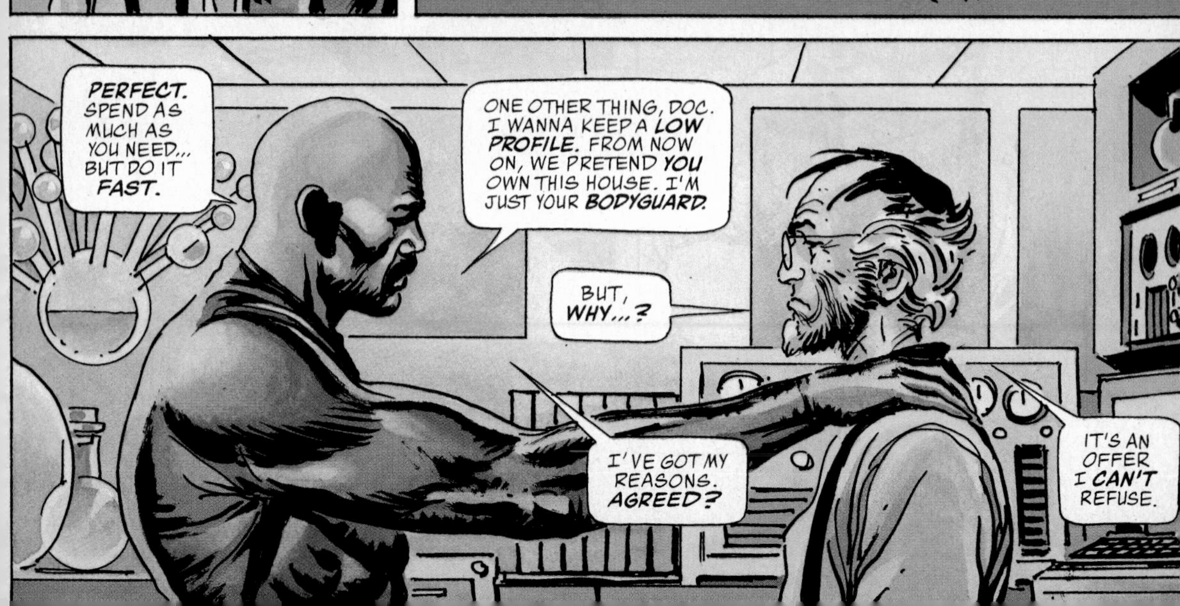

NOT LONG AFTER...
HANDZ, YOU'RE WORTH A FORTUNE. YOU HAVE EVERYTHING YOU WANT.
WHY WON'T YOU... LET ME GO?
'CUZ I AIN'T GOT EVERY-THING I WANT.
NOT TILL YOU SAY YA'LL MARRY ME.
I BEEN PATIENT ALL THIS TIME... WAITIN' FOR YA TO COME TO YER SENSES. NOW... I'M THROUGH WAITIN'!

YOU GOT ONE HOUR TO MAKE UP YER MIND. IT'S EITHER ME--OR A LEAD KIMONO.
'CUZ IF I CAN'T HAVE YA-- NO ONE WILL!

YOU CLAIM TO LOVE ME... YET... YOU THREATEN ME?
YEAH. YOU GOT THAT RIGHT.

THIS IS THE BUILDING.
THE CHOPPER'S SET ON AUTO-PILOT.

IT'S TURNING TO RETURN TO BASE.
HERE'S WHERE I SEE IF THE DOC DID HIS JOB RIGHT.

THE DOC DID IT!

AS LONG AS THERE'S **AIR CURRENTS** UNDER ME... I CAN **GLIDE** LIKE A **BAT**.

I GOTTA LEARN HOW TO SLOW MY DESCENT...

THEY MIGHT **HEAR** IT WHEN MY FEET TOUCH DOWN.

IT--IT'S **BATMAN** THE WRESTLER, BOSS.
**GET RID'A HIM.** NOBODY CRASHES IN HERE.
I SEEN HIM RASSLE, BOSS...
...M-MAYBE WE OUGHTA GO EASY ON 'IM.
I DON'T GO EASY ON **NOBODY.** NO **TWO-BIT WRESTLER** CAN SCARE **HANDZ HORGUM!**

AIN'T **NOBODY** GOT A CHANCE AGAINST **MY FISTS!**
I GOT THE **NOTCHES** ON MY GLOVES T'**PROVE** IT!
GOT NEWS FOR YOU, HANDZ... YOU'RE NOT UP AGAINST A **HELPLESS TEENAGER** NOW.

WHADDAYA TALKIN' ABOU--

UMMPH!
DON'T WORRY... YOU'LL GET THE MESSAGE.

SPANNG
LUCKY FOR ME DOC'S **KEVLAR** WORKS!
KRAK
TAKKA-TAK
**STOP SHOOTIN'!** I WANNA TEAR 'IM APART **MYSELF!**
YOU HEARD THE MAN... WE DON'T WANNA BE INTERRUPTED.
GOTTA **MOVE**... BEFORE HE TURNS AROUND.

IT AIN'T SAFE T'TURN YER BACK ON ME, SUCKER!
THUD

KRUNK

IF NOT FOR MY MASK'S PADDING... I'D BE HISTORY!
IT--IT AIN'T POSSIBLE. Y'CAN'T... STILL BE STANDIN'.

NO? C'MON-- CHECK ME OUT FOR YOURSELF.
I'LL KILL YA!

I'LL CRUSH YA LIKE A GRAPE!
FORGET IT. THIS TIME MY BACK'S NOT TURNED.
A GUY LEARNS A LOT IN THE RING. SOME-TIMES YOU DO BETTER LAYIN' DOWN.
N-NO...
OOONOOOOOOOOOOOOOOOOOO

THAT'S FOR MY PARENTS, SLIME-BALL...
...AND FOR ME.

I PRAYED FOR SOMETHING TO FREE ME FROM HANDZ. BUT NOT THIS. NOT MURDER.
NITA!

WHOEVER YOU REALLY ARE, YOUR MASK DOESN'T GIVE YOU THE RIGHT TO KILL.

NITA... YOU DON'T UNDER-STAND...

H-HOW DO YOU KNOW MY NAME?
I CAN'T TELL YOU--YET.
SHE'S GOT NO JOB, NO PLACE TO GO. I'LL HAVE GRANT CON-TACT HER--SAY HE NEEDS A SECRETARY.
NO MATTER WHAT SHE THINKS OF ME... I WANT HER IN MY LIFE.

LATER THAT NIGHT, A SPECIAL SERVICE IS HELD AT THE CHURCH OF ETERNAL EMPOWERMENT...
I HAVE SUMMONED YOU FOR A PURPOSE, MY FAITHFUL ONES.
OUR MASTER PLAN IS ABOUT TO REACH FRUITION.

BE WARNED... ANOTHER PLAYER HAS UNWITTINGLY ENTERED THE GAME. HE IS KNOWN AS--THE BATMAN.
BUT HIS POWER IS AS NOTHING COMPARED TO MINE.
AS EASILY AS I HAVE CREATED HIS IMAGE...
...WITH THE MEREST SHRUG, I MAKE IT VANISH!
AND, AS EASILY AS I DESTROYED HIS IMAGE... SO SHALL THE BATMAN BE DESTROYED.
NOW... LET THE GAME BEGIN!

ON THE STREET
BONG
BONG
BONG
LOS DO LIT
LOS A DO LIT
BONG
BONG
BONG
BATMAN STRIK
News
BATMAN STRIKES
Los Angeles News
CH OF
ERNAL
LWERMENT
AY'S SERMON:
ATMAN STRIKES
BATMAN STRIKES
Los Angeles News

BATMAN STRIKES
Los Angeles News

BATMAN STRIKES

BATMA
STRIKE
Los Angeles News

Los Angeles News

HOT BAGELS

Los Angeles News

MMM!
86
Los Angeles News
BAH!
86
Los Angeles News

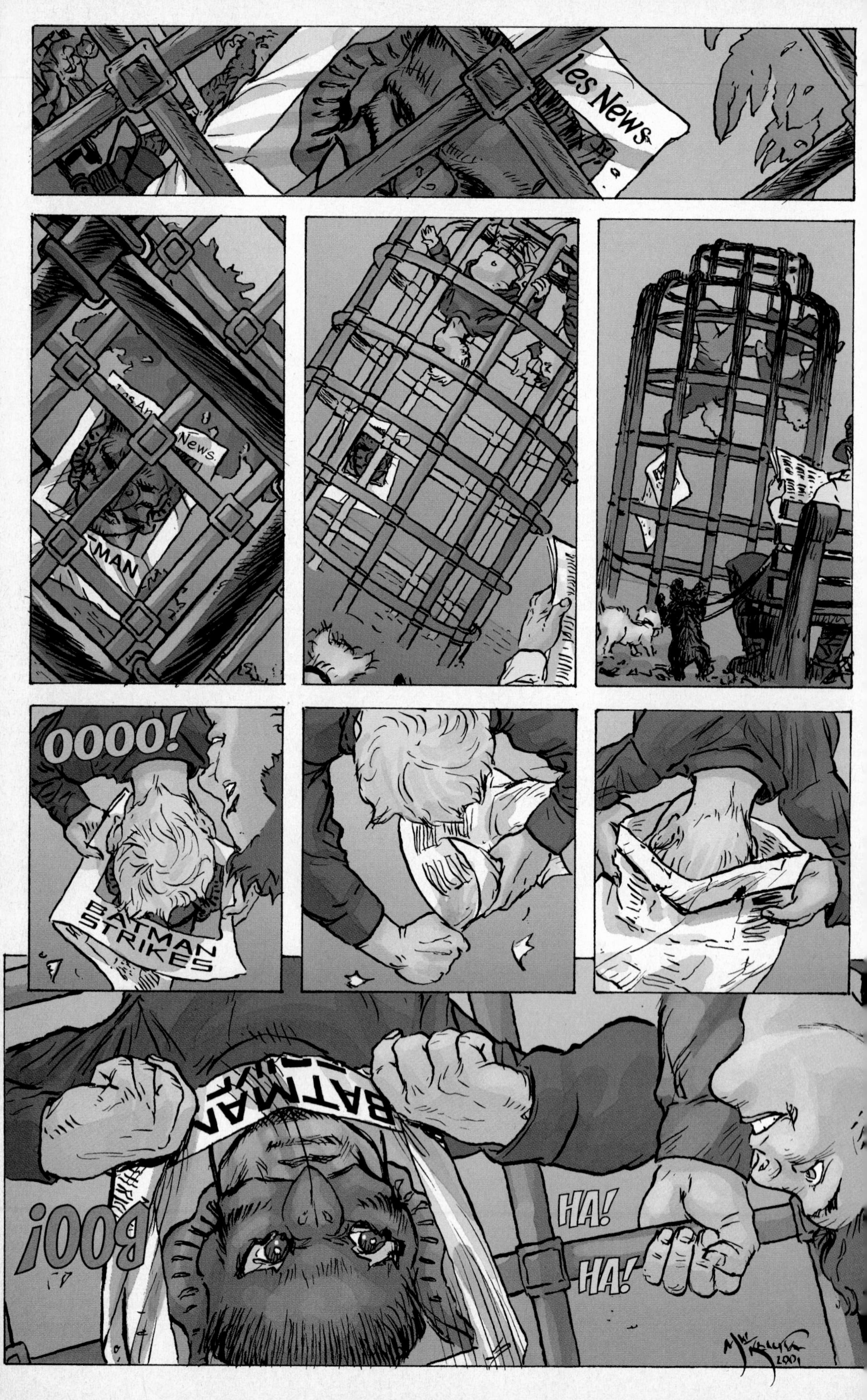

les News.
News.
MAN
OOOO!
BATMAN
STRIKES
BATMAN
BOO!
HA!
HA!

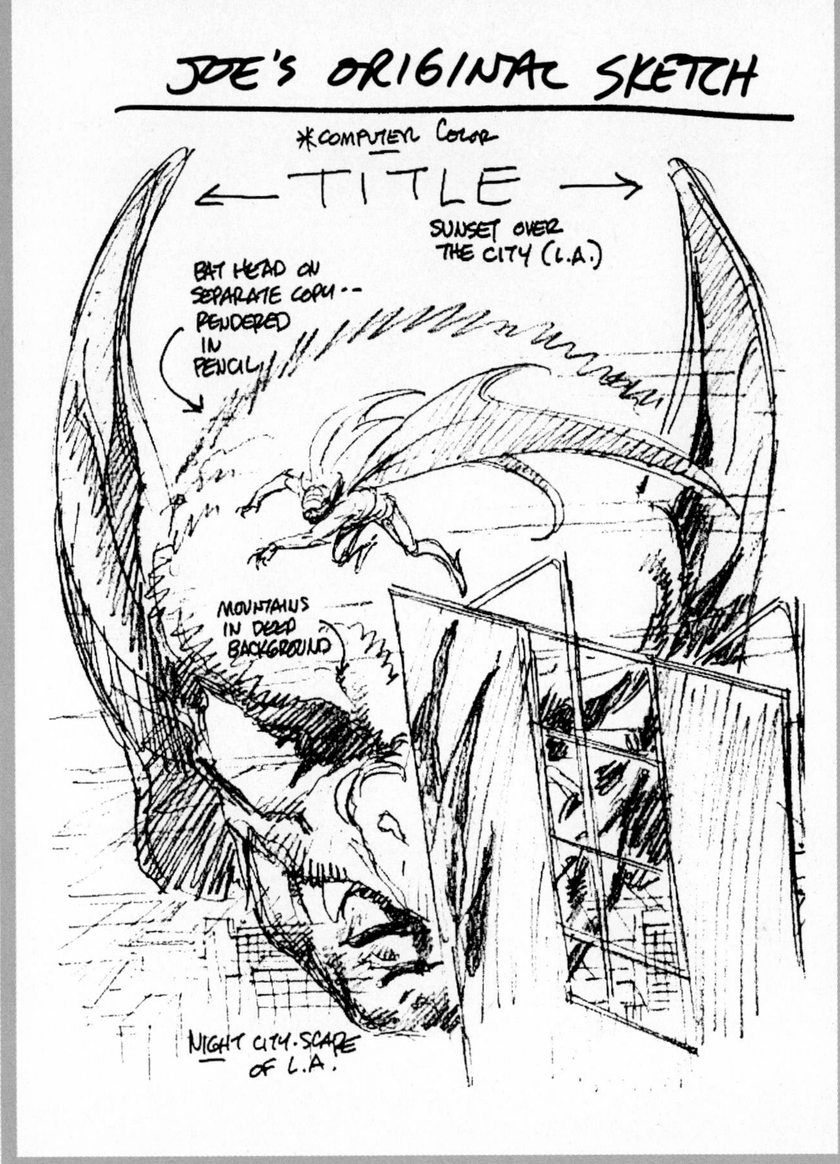


It was an extremely gratifying experience for me to draw the Batman story in the JUST IMAGINE... series. There are a number of reasons for my very positive reaction, some of which were part of the initial proposal that was brought to me.

First, I'd illustrated some [traditional] Batman stories and covers in the past, and it's always an interesting challenge for me to revisit a character to see if I've learned some things — to add some things — to flesh the character out a bit more than in my earlier attempts.

Then, I was told that this Batman story was going to be a "new take" on the character, and was to be written by Stan Lee.

I'd known Stan for years and had occasion to be with him at conventions and other functions. I was well aware of his accomplishments and reputation in our field. Those were reasons enough for me to become involved in the project. Add to that the fact that this Batman was to be a black man, an ex-con, a pro wrestler, also

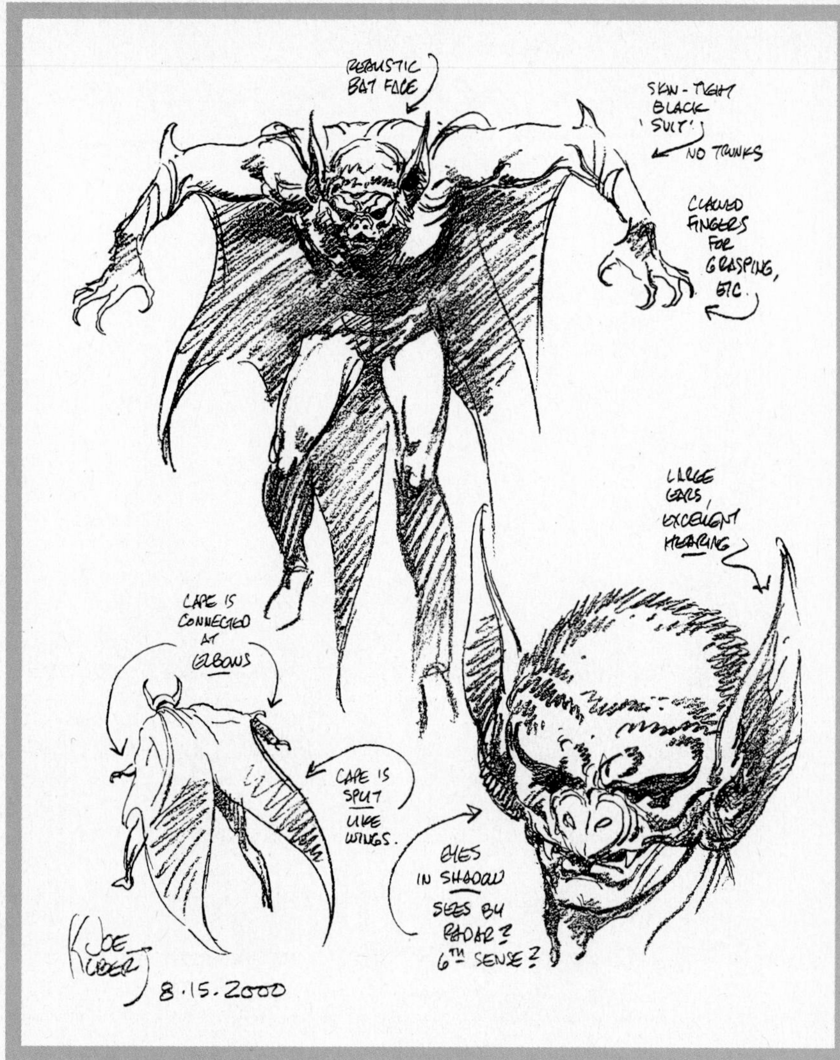


equipped with the ability to glide through the air, and I don't know of any cartoonist who wouldn't be excited about the prospect.

This was the first time I'd had the opportunity to work with Stan Lee. Stan had always been the *stan*dard (please excuse the pun) bearer of Marvel Comics, while my involvement in past years has been with DC. I wondered how we'd get along, especially since Stan lives in California and I in New Jersey.

Any concerns about working with Stan were almost immediately dispelled. A few phone calls and some amiable conversation, and it was clear to me that Stan looked forward to my involvement and graphic contributions, just as I looked forward to illustrating his JUST IMAGINE... Batman story.

It was an enjoyable and rewarding experience, and I look forward to any future "next time" with Stan the Man.

**— Joe Kubert**

AGES AGO, THERE WAS A TIME OF WONDER, A TIME OF MYSTERY AND MIRACLES.
COME BACK WITH US TO SUCH A TIME.
TO THE LEGENDARY LAKE TITICACA, IN THE LAND MEN CALL PERU.
COME BACK TO THAT MAGICAL MOMENT WHEN THE INCAN SUN GOD ROARED A FATEFUL COMMAND...
AND LO, HIS MIGHTY SON, MANCO CAPAC, AROSE FROM THE LAKE...
... WITH BUT ONE BURNING PURPOSE, ONE UNSHAKABLE GOAL...
...TO CREATE THE LEGENDARY CITY OF CUZCO, FOR THE GLORY OF HIS FATHER.
MANCO CAPAC WAS GIVEN AN ENCHANTED STAFF OF GOLD...
...TO PLUNGE INTO THE GROUND, WHERE E'RE HE WALKED.
WHEN THE GOLDEN STAFF SANK ALL THE WAY...
...THEN HE WOULD KNOW HE HAD FOUND THE FATEFUL SITE!

WHO CAN SAY HOW FAR HE JOURNEYED, HOW LONG HE SEARCHED?
TIME AND DISTANCE HAD NO MEANING FOR MANCO CAPAC.
PROTECTED FROM ANY FORM OF EVIL BY THE GOLDEN STAFF, HE NEVER FALTERED AS HE LED HIS FAITHFUL FOLLOWERS.
NO MATTER THE UNSPEAKABLE HORRORS THEY FACED, THEY FOLLOWED THE SUN GOD'S CHOSEN ONE...
UNTIL, AT LAST...
THE GOLDEN STAFF SANK ALL THE WAY INTO THE WELCOMING EARTH!
THE QUEST WAS ENDED!
THE FABLED CITY OF CUZCO WAS BORN!
NEVER HAD THERE BEEN A PLACE SO WONDROUS; A PLACE OF BEAUTY, PEACE AND PLENTY.
BUT THAT WAS AGES AGO.

TODAY, TIME HAS RAVAGED THE GLORY OF CUZCO.
FORSAKEN AND FORGOTTEN ARE ITS ONCE-FABLED SPLENDORS.
BUT ITS DESTINY IS NOT YET FULFILLED.
PELIGRO
WHICH SADDENS THE HEART OF MARIA MENDOZA.
IT'S SO HARD TO BELIEVE THAT THIS WAS ONCE THE JEWEL OF THE INCAN EMPIRE.
TODAY, NOTHING REMAINS BUT RUINS.
AND EVEN THE RUINS NOW SUFFER THE FINAL INDIGNITY...
AS THEY'RE DESTROYED BY THE RICH AND POWERFUL ARMANDO GUITEZ, WHOSE MEN KEEP DIGGING AND SEARCHING FOR BURIED TREASURE.
GUITEZ CARES NOTHING FOR OUR PROUD HERITAGE.
OR FOR THE SUFFERING OF THE POOR FARMERS HE KEEPS DRIVING FROM THEIR LAND.
MARIA'S REVERIE IS SUDDENLY BROKEN, AS...
YOU SHOULD NOT BE HERE!

THIS PROPERTY IS OFF-LIMITS TO TOURISTS.
IT'S A SCIENTIFIC, ARCHAEOLOGICAL DIG FINANCED BY AMANDO GUITEZ.
HOW DARE YOU MENTION SCIENCE IN THE SAME BREATH AS ARMANDO GUITEZ!
I DESPISE HIM AND ALL HE STANDS FOR!
HE'S WILLING TO DESTROY OUR SACRED GROUND AND PLUNDER OUR HERITAGE IN HIS GREEDY LUST FOR BURIED TREASURE!
YOU'RE QUITE A CRUSADER, AREN'T YOU?
AND A LOVELY ONE, AT THAT.
LOOK, MY NAME'S STEVE TREVOR. I CAME ALL THE WAY FROM LOS ANGELES TO WORK ON THIS DIG.
THEN YOU'RE AN ARCHAEOLOGIST?
RIGHT, AND I'M TRYING TO KEEP GUITEZ FROM DOING TOO MUCH DAMAGE.
BUT HE'LL SELL OUR HISTORIC TREASURES TO ANYONE WHO'LL PAY THE PRICE!
THAT'S WHY I'M TRYING TO SEE THAT THEY'RE BOUGHT ONLY BY MUSEUMS.
BUT YOU SHOULDN'T BE HERE...
IT'S TOO DANGEROUS.
DANGEROUS? I'M NOT AFRAID OF GUITEZ.
IT ISN'T HE WHO'S THE DANGER.
LISTEN! DID YOU HEAR THAT?

IT SOUNDED LIKE HEAVY FOOTSTEPS! BUT WHO--?

HURRY! MY JEEP'S NEARBY.

BY THE WAY, I DON'T KNOW YOUR NAME...

DON'T CHANGE THE SUBJECT. I WANT TO KNOW WHAT IT IS YOU'RE AFRAID OF!

LATER, IN THE SLEEPY VILLAGE OF SANTA ATALAYA...

WAIT. YOU MUST BE HUNGRY.

HOW ABOUT HAVING BREAKFAST WITH ME?

I CAN'T--

I MUST SPEAK WITH MY FATHER!

SHE'S SO LOVELY, SO IDEALISTIC...

SHE MUST HATE ME FOR WORKING FOR GUITEZ!

FATHER! YOU'RE SANTA ATALAYA'S OFFICIAL JUEZ!*

HOW CAN YOU LET THAT HORRIBLE ARMANDO GUITEZ DESECRATE OUR HISTORIC SHRINES?

FATHER! PLEASE ANSWER ME!

*"JUEZ" = JUDGE.

I'M TRYING TO FIND THE WORDS, MY CHILD.

IS IT--BECAUSE OF WHAT HAPPENED YEARS AGO?

YES, MARIA. BUT I NEVER TOLD YOU THE WHOLE STORY.

TELL ME NOW.

IT BEGAN ON THE DAY YOU WERE BORN...
A POOR FARMER, BRINGING HIS WIFE AND NEW BABY HOME FROM THE HOSPITAL--
--WAS STOPPED BY BANDITOS!
"THEY WANTED MONEY. HE HAD NONE.
"THEY DIDN'T BELIEVE HIM. THEY FOUGHT.
"A SHOT RANG OUT!
"THE FARMER'S ADORED WIFE--FELL DEAD."
IN THOSE FEW ACCURSED SECONDS, THAT BABY LOST HER MOTHER--AND I, MY WIFE!
YOU WERE THAT FARMER!

"THE STORY IS NOT YET ENDED.
"HEARING THE SHOT, THE POLICIA ARRIVED.
"THE KILLERS FLED.
"I THOUGHT I WAS SAVED.
"I WAS WRONG!"
GIVE US YOUR MONEY AND WE WILL FIND YOUR WIFE'S KILLER.
THEY LEFT ME NO MONEY.
THEN WE WILL TAKE YOUR TRUCK.
"LATER I SAW THEM LAUGHING-- DIVIDING THE SPOILS!
"ON THAT DAY, I SWORE A SACRED OATH...
"NEVER AGAIN WOULD I BE A VICTIM!"

YOU, MY DAUGHTER, WILL BE PROTECTED--
--IF IT MEANS MY SIGNING A PACT WITH THE DEVIL!
BUT, FATHER, GUITEZ IS A DEVIL!
WE WILL SAY NO MORE!
I HAVE BORNE THIS BURDEN FOR TOO LONG.
DO YOU THINK I FEEL NO SHAME IN SERVING SUCH A MAN?
MY POOR, TORTURED FATHER.
Ah, THE ELUSIVE MARIA MENDOZA.
WHY HAVE YOU BEEN AVOIDING ME LATELY, MY LOVELY?
NOT LATELY, SEÑOR GUITEZ--
ALWAYS!
BUT THINK WHAT I CAN OFFER YOU, MY PRETTY ONE.
I AM NEITHER YOUR LOVELY NOR YOUR PRETTY!
I DESPISE YOU AND EVERYTHING YOU STAND FOR!
JUST AS I HAVE MADE HER FATHER MY OBEDIENT PUPPET--
--SO SHALL I MAKE MARIA MINE!
THE POLICIA REFUSE TO PROTECT US, JUDGE MENDOZA.
THEY DO NOT BELIEVE A GIANT DEMON IS ATTACKING OUR HOMES AND FARMS.
AND ARMANDO GUITEZ TELLS THEM NOT TO HELP US!
HE SEEKS TO DRIVE US FROM OUR FARMS!
PRAY CONTINUE, FRIEND. YOUR STORY TOUCHES MY HEART.

SURELY YOU KNOW I AM THE FARMER'S BEST FRIEND.
EVERY FIBER OF MY BEING FEELS YOUR SORROW AND PAIN.
I--I THANK YOU FOR THAT, SEÑOR.
WE--NEVER KNEW...
WE ALWAYS--FEARED YOU.
...YOU MUST BE TAUGHT NEVER TO SPEAK ILL OF YOUR BETTERS.
NOOOO, SEÑOR!
I KNOW THAT LOOK ON GUITEZ'S FACE.
I PITY THE POOR, UNSUSPECTING FARMER.
BUT, EVEN THOUGH IT WILL PAIN ME GREATLY...
DON'T DO IT, GUITEZ. CAN YOU NOT SHOW SOME HUMAN COMPASSION--JUST ONCE?
NOW, MY BRAVE ONES, TEACH THAT IMPUDENT FOOL A MUCH-NEEDED LESSON.
LET ALL SANTA ATALAYA BEHOLD THE FATE OF THOSE WHO INCUR THE WRATH OF ARMANDO GUITEZ!
SNAP
EL PRESIDENTE! ONLY HE CAN HELP US!
A MESSAGE MUST BE SENT!
MADRE DIOS! THE GUARDS HAVE SEEN ME!
STOP WHERE YOU ARE!
I AM LOST!
BUT I WILL NOT MEET THE FATE OF THE OTHERS.
IF I MUST DIE...
LET IT BE--
--WITH DIGNITY!
BLAMM

GUARDS! DISPOSE OF THAT CARRION.
THE POOR MAN SHOT HIMSELF!
SI! AND NOW HE LITTERS THE STREETS OF OUR FAIR CITY.

YOU HAVE BEEN TOO LENIENT, MENDOZA.
YOU MUST NOT ALLOW TROUBLEMAKERS IN YOUR COURTROOM.
DOES NOT EVERY MAN DESERVE A HEARING?
NOT THOSE WHO OPPOSE ME!

YOU WILL NOW COME WITH US!
SEÑOR GUITEZ IS NOT PLEASED WITH YOUR ATTITUDE.

IT IS NOT WISE TO DISPLEASE SEÑOR GUITEZ.
320
POLICIA

WHERE WILL THEY TAKE OUR JUEZ?
IT IS BEST NOT TO KNOW.
THE POLICIA! THEY HAVE MY FATHER!

SEÑOR TREVOR! GRACIAS A DIOS, I HAVE FOUND YOU!
I NEED YOUR HELP!
DOES IT HAVE TO DO WITH THAT RUCKUS AT THE COURTHOUSE?
THEY HAVE TAKEN MY FATHER!

I HAD A HUNCH YOU WERE MARIA, THE JUDGE'S DAUGHTER.
PLEASE! WILL YOU HELP ME?
WHY NOT?

LET'S JUST SAY SEÑOR GUITEZ IS EXPECTING ME.
MY BUSINESS IS--PERSONAL.
YOU ARE A MAN OF THE WORLD.
I'M SURE YOU UNDERSTAND.
NICE TRY, SEÑORITA. BUT I KNOW ALL OF SEÑOR GUITEZ'S FEMALE, eh, "GUESTS."
YOU ARE NOT ONE OF THEM.
DON'T SWEAT IT, AMIGO. SHE'S WITH ME.
GUITEZ INDUSTRIES
Steve Trevor
ID: 7952894A
B
WHAT A FOOL I WAS!
I THOUGHT YOU WERE JUST AN ARCHAEOLOGIST.
I DIDN'T SUSPECT YOU WERE ONE OF GUITEZ'S MEN!
HEY, WAIT A MINUTE, LADY. I WAS JUST TRYIN' TO-- UMFF!
STAY AWAY! I'VE GOT TO FIND MY FATHER!

WOW! SHE SURE AIN'T SHY ABOUT EXPRESSING HER FEEL- INGS!
BUT OKAY, I CAN TAKE A HINT.
I'LL GIVE HER HER OWN SPACE.
THERE'S MY FATHER, WITH SOME OF THE PEASANTS.
I TELL YOU, GUITEZ, YOU CAN NO LONGER OPENLY DEFY THE LAW!
YOU ARE WRONG, MENDOZA.
I AM THE LAW!
YOU WILL OBEY ME, OR ELSE!
BLAMM!
PERHAPS THAT WILL BRING YOU TO YOUR SENSES!
YOU--SHOT THAT FARMER --IN COLD BLOOD!
SI! I AM TIRED OF PROTESTS, OF COMPLAINTS.
NOW WHAT DO YOU HAVE TO SAY?
SOMEONE MUST STOP YOU, GUITEZ! I'LL GO TO THE GOVERNOR!

ON'T NK SO.
YOU KILLED MY FATHER!
OBVIOUSLY, MY DEAR.

YOU ARRIVED JUST IN TIME TO BID OUR LATE JUEZ A FOND FAREWELL.
BUT MY BRIDE-TO-BE MUST NOT BE BURDENED WITH SORDID MATTERS!
NOW THAT YOU ARE HERE--
--I SHALL NEVER LET YOU GO.
YOU MURDEROUS DEVIL!
I'D DIE A THOUSAND DEATHS BEFORE I'D LET YOU TOUCH ME!
FOOL! IF YOU SHOOT HER, HE'LL KILL YOU!

IT DOESN'T MATTER WHAT HAPPENS TO ME!
BUT I'VE GOT TO ESCAPE-- TO AVENGE MY FATHER!

QUIET! DON'T MAKE A SOUND! DON'T EVEN BREATHE!

TRUST ME! I KNOW WHERE YOU CAN HIDE!

I FOUND HER. GUITEZ WILL REWARD ME GENER-OUSLY!

WE'LL GO TO THE EXCAVATION.
YOU WON'T BELIEVE YOUR EYES DOWN THERE!

I LEARNED THE REAL REASON GUITEZ HAS BEEN EXCAVATING THIS SITE.
IT ALL GOES BACK TO THE ANCIENT LEGEND OF THE SUN GOD.
THERE IS POWER HERE--AND INDESCRIBABLE EVIL--MORE TERRIBLE THAN ANYONE CAN IMAGINE!
THIS IS PART OF THE LOST TEMPLES OF THE INCAS.

IT WAS HERE THAT MANCO, THE SUN GOD, USED HIS GOLDEN STAFF OF LIGHT TO IMPRISON THE EVIL SPIRITS WHICH THREATENED MANKIND.
THIS IS WHY GUITEZ TRIES TO DRIVE THE PEASANTS FROM THE LAND!
WITHIN THIS TEMPLE HE SEEKS THE RUNES OF ABSOLUTE POWER--

POWER ENOUGH TO TOPPLE CIVILIZATION ITSELF!

LUCKILY, I MANAGED TO SHIP THE TWO MOST POTENT RUNES TO LOS ANGELES--
WHERE GUITEZ WON'T BE ABLE TO GET HIS HANDS ON THEM.

BUT I THINK HE SUSPECTS WHAT I'VE DONE!

MORE THAN JUST "SUSPECT"--
I KNOW!
THE RUNE!
I DROPPED IT!
DO YOU BELIEVE IN FATE, LITTLE SPARROW?
YOUR FATHER IS GONE.
YOUR ERSTWHILE PROTECTOR IS GONE.
IT SEEMS YOU ARE FATED TO BE MINE.
BUT, EVEN AS GUITEZ GLOATS...
OF COURSE, YOU HAVE ANOTHER CHOICE.
BUT GUNSHOT WOUNDS CAN BE AWFULLY MESSY.
AT THAT INSTANT...

THE LEGENDS ARE TRUE!
THE RUNE HAS OPENED!
AN EVIL SPIRIT IS RELEASED!
IF WE ARE DOOMED-- I PRAY THAT YOU BE THE FIRST TO DIE!
THAT CANNOT HAPPEN!
I AM ITS MASTER!
IT WAS I WHO UNLEASHED IT!

RUN, MARIA.
I'M DONE FOR-- BUT YOU-- MUST LIVE...
LIVE? FOR WHAT?
EVERYWHERE-- DEATH--ALL AROUND ME!
COME TO ME, THING OF EVIL!
COME AND LEARN THAT ARMANDO GUITEZ IS YOUR MASTER!

SEIZE ME!
GRASP ME IN YOUR FOUL EMBRACE!
LET ME FEEL THE EVIL FLOWING THROUGH MY VEINS!
GIVE ME YOUR RAGE! GIVE ME YOUR POWER!
LET ME BECOME WHAT I AM DESTINED TO BE!
I HAVE WON!
THE POWER-- AND THE EVIL-- ARE MINE!

BUT WHY SHOULD I STOP NOW?
THERE, ON THE GROUND --ANOTHER RUNE!
ALL I NEED DO IS SMASH IT!

IF I SEE ANY MORE I'LL GO MAD!
I'VE GOT TO ESCAPE THIS LIVING NIGHTMARE!
WHO HAS DISTURBED MY SLUMBER OF CENTURIES?
WHO DARES VIOLATE THE SACRED RUNES?
I DARE!
I, WHO AM NOW YOUR MASTER!
FOR THE FIRST TIME IN AGES, I SENSE EVIL GREATER THAN MINE!
AND POWER ENOUGH TO MATCH THAT EVIL!
ATTACK ME-- IF YOU DARE!
I DARE!

...MARIA BEGINS TO REGAIN CONSCIOUSNESS AT THE BOTTOM OF THE MYSTIC SITE.
WHILE, FAR BELOW...
AS THE AWESOME BATTLE RAGES...
SLOWLY, AGONIZINGLY, THE POWER OF GUITEZ BEGINS TO PREVAIL.
IT--IT WASN'T A DREAM!
THE NIGHTMARE --IS REAL!
I'VE DONE IT!
I'VE BEATEN HIM!
HIS POWER, TOO, IS MINE!
NOTHING ON EARTH CAN OPPOSE ME NOW!
ALL THAT REMAINS IS THE TWO MISSING RUNES--SOMEWHERE IN LOS ANGELES!
I'LL MAKE THEM MINE--AFTER I CRUSH THE ENTIRE CITY!

I'M GOING MAD. I HEAR VOICES.
THE ANOINTED ONE HAS COME.
LET THE RITUAL BEGIN.
WHO IS IT? WHO'S THERE?
WHO'S SAYING THAT?
HAVE NO FEAR.
HEED THESE WORDS.
STRETCH OUT YOUR HAND...
WHAT IS THAT--?
IT-- APPEARED OUT OF NOWHERE!
SEIZE YOU NOW THE GOLDEN STAFF.
THE DEED IS DONE!
THE PROPHECY FULFILLED!

A BLINDING BURST OF LIGHT ILLUMINATES THE SKY...
IT CAME FROM THE EXCAVATION.
GOOD! THE WHOLE PLACE CAN GO UP IN FLAMES FOR ALL I CARE.
BUT IT IS NOT THE BLAZE OF DESTRUCTION.
IT IS THE GLEAMING AURA OF REBIRTH, OF REDEMPTIVE POWER, UNLEASHED AT LAST!

MY PRIVATE PLANE IS READY, AS ALWAYS.
THEY MAY NOT RECOGNIZE ME...
...BUT NO ONE WILL DARE TRY TO STOP ME.
STAY BACK. I WANT NO CREW. ONLY THE PILOT.
THERE'S FUEL ENOUGH TO REACH LOS ANGELES.

YOU MUST REST HERE WHILE I GO FOR HELP.
NO. THERE'S NO TIME. I'VE--ONLY SECONDS LEFT. ONLY SECONDS--TO MAKE YOU UNDERSTAND.
YOUR DESTINY WAS SET CENTURIES AGO WHEN MANCO CAPAC BURIED HIS GOLDEN STAFF IN THE ENCHANTED VALLEY OF CUZCO.
YOU ARE THE CHOSEN OF THE SUN GOD. YOU ARE--THE PROTECTRESS OF EARTH!
THERE IS--SO MUCH EVIL IN THE WORLD--SO MUCH--FOR YOU TO DO...
YOU--MUST NOT FAIL. YOU ARE--THE SUN GODDESS...
HE'S DEAD.
SO MANY LIVES--LOST.
NOT EVEN A SUN GODDESS CAN BRING THEM BACK.
I DON'T WANT TO BE PROTECTRESS OF EARTH. I'M NOT A GODDESS.
I'M A GIRL--A GIRL WHO'S LOST HER FATHER--WHO HASN'T EVEN HAD TIME TO MOURN.

THERE'S ONLY ONE ANSWER TO EVERYTHING THAT'S HAPPENED...
I WAS AFRAID TO BELIEVE IT. I COULDN'T FACE IT.
BUT NOW I MUST!
I MUST LEARN TO LIVE WITH ONE HORRIBLE FACT--
I'VE LOST MY MIND! I'M TOTALLY--INSANE!
NO, MARIA MENDOZA, YOURS IS THE CLEAREST MIND OF ALL.
IT IS NOT BY CHANCE THAT YOU WERE CHOSEN.
YOURS IS THE SPIRIT, COMPASSION AND COURAGE WE HAVE SOUGHT FOR CENTURIES.
DO NOT CONTEST THE WILL OF THE GODS.
SEIZE NOW THE GOLDEN STAFF--AND BEHOLD THE WONDERS THAT SHALL ENSUE.

BY TOUCHING THE GOLDEN STAFF, YOU SEAL THE BARGAIN...
...AND THE SUN GODDESS LIVES ONCE MORE!
IF THAT IS TO BE MY FATE--THEN LET ME TOUCH IT!
IT IS DONE!
AND NOW ...THE TRAINING...
THE GOLDEN STAFF IS YOUR KEY TO THE HEAVENS.
WITH IT, YOU MAY FLY AT WILL.
IN THE AIR, NONE CAN SEE IT BUT YOU.
IT WILL SEEM AS THOUGH I'M FLYING BY MYSELF.
YOU HAVE ONLY TO THINK OF A SPEED, A DESTINATION.
THE STAFF WILL DO ALL ELSE.
AND SHOULD YOU LET GO, IT WILL DRIFT DOWN AT YOUR SIDE...
...SO THAT YOU MAY GRASP IT AGAIN, AT WILL.
SEE HOW EASILY YOU CAN FLOAT DOWN TO EARTH.
WHEN YOU WISH TO ASSUME YOUR NORMAL IDENTITY...
...MERELY **THINK** THAT DESIRE --AND YOUR STAFF WILL TRANSFORM INTO A GOLDEN BRACELET.
EACH TIME YOU TOUCH IT, THE CHANGE WILL OCCUR.
GUITEZ! HE MUSTN'T GET AWAY!

A PRIVATE PLANE APPROACHES LOS ANGELES AIRPORT FROM SOUTH AMERICA...
I HAVEN'T HEARD FROM SEÑOR GUITEZ SINCE WE TOOK OFF.
SIR, IS EVERYTHING ALL RIGHT BACK THERE--?
DON'T OPEN THAT DOOR! DON'T TURN AROUND!
SORRY, SIR. I DIDN'T MEAN TO--TO--
WELL, NO MATTER. WE'RE ALMOST THERE, ANYWAY.
SO IT'S TIME TO PRACTICE MY KILLING SKILLS!
WHY BOTHER LANDING AT AN AIRPORT--
--WHEN I CAN CRASH DOWN ANYWHERE!

EVENING IN LOS ANGELES. ON FAMOUS MULHOLLAND DRIVE THE SPORTS CAR OF MIKE WILLARD, WRITER/EDITOR OF "THE NATIONAL EXPOSER," COMES TO A SUDDEN STOP...
HOLLYWOOD
SOMETHING EXPLODED DOWN THERE NEAR GRIFFITH PARK!
LUCKY I'VE GOT MY NIGHT-VISION CAMERA BINOC!
IT'S LIKE SOMETHING OUT OF "ALIEN" OR "PREDATOR!"
I DIDN'T KNOW THEY WERE SHOOTING ANOTHER MONSTER FLICK!
NOW SOMETHING ELSE IS ZOOMING THROUGH THE SKY!
WHAT KIND OF PLANE--?
NO! IT'S NOT A PLANE!
IT'S GLEAMING LIKE A GOLDEN MISSILE--BUT IT'S NOT A MISSILE!
IT'S--IT'S A--NO! IT CAN'T BE!
I'VE SEEN SPECIAL EFFECTS--BUT NEVER ANYTHING LIKE THAT!
DO NOT FEAR. I WILL SUBDUE THE MONSTER!

GUITEZ IS NO LONGER HUMAN!

Church of Eternal Empower

BUT I WONDER--AM I?

YOU KILLED MY FATHER--AND OTHER INNOCENT BEINGS!
YOU WILL NEVER KILL AGAIN!
NO GARISHLY COSTUMED FEMALE CAN STOP ME!
I HAVE THE POWER OF THE MYSTIC RUNES!
IF THE SUN GOD HIMSELF COULD NOT DESTROY THE POWER OF EVIL--
--THEN NEITHER WILL YOU!

INSTINCTIVELY, MARIA RAISES HER GLEAM-ING SHIELD...
...AS SHARDS OF DAZZLING ENERGY BURST FORTH...
...REDUCING THE GIANT BOULDER TO RUBBLE BEFORE IT CAN STRIKE THE GODDESS
WITH THE SPEED OF A COMET, THE FORCE OF A GALE, SHE TWISTS THE SHARDS INTO A MIGHTY CABLE...
IT FEELS AS THOUGH I'VE DONE THIS MANY TIMES BEFORE.
HAVE THERE BEEN OTHER GODDESSES IN AGES PAST?
AM I BUT ANOTHER IN A LONG AND END-LESS CHAIN?

FEMALE FOOL! A CABLE HAS **TWO** ENDS!
BY GRABBING MINE I CAN HURL YOU AWAY LIKE A HELPLESS RAG DOLL!
YOUR STRENGTH MAY BE THE EQUAL OF MINE.
BUT I POSSESS ONE POWER THAT IS DENIED TO YOU!
THE POWER OF FLIGHT!
EVEN IN THE AIR-- THE CABLE HAS TWO ENDS!
AND I'LL CLIMB TO YOU FROM MINE!

I WANTED YOU TO CLIMB CLOSE ENOUGH--
--FOR ME TO STOMP YOUR FIENDISH FACE!
EACH BLOW IS FOR THOSE INNOCENT YOUNG MEN YOU KILLED!

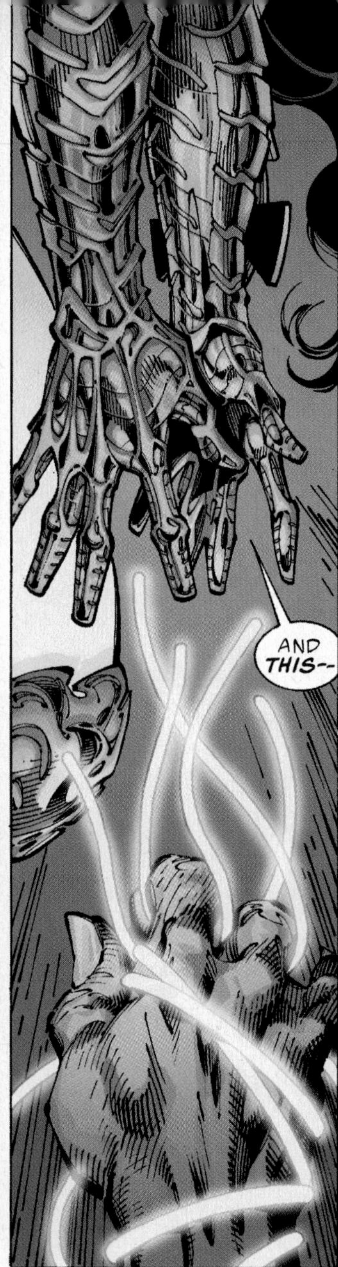
AND THIS--

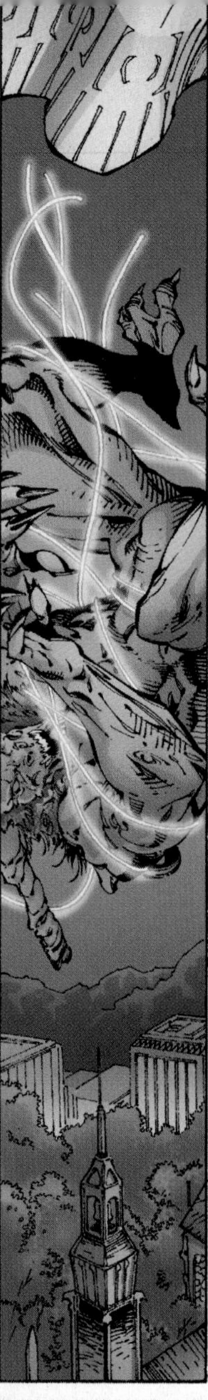

--IS FOR MY FATHER!

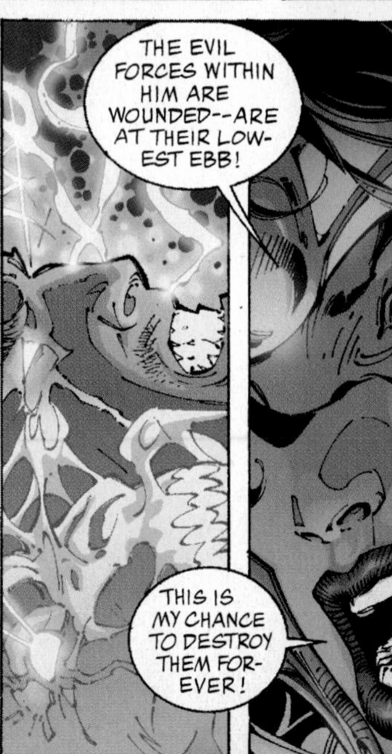
THE EVIL FORCES WITHIN HIM ARE WOUNDED--ARE AT THEIR LOWEST EBB!
THIS IS MY CHANCE TO DESTROY THEM FOREVER!

BY THE POWER OF MY GOLDEN STAFF, LET THE MONSTER BE GONE --FOREVER!
THE GODS HAVE SPOKEN! THE DEED IS DONE!
IF I WASN'T HALLUCINATING, I JUST WITNESSED THE GREATEST STORY OF THE CENTURY!
CENTURY? HELL, IT COULD BE THE GREAT-EST STORY OF ALL TIME!
GOTTA GET TO MY OFFICE, FAST!
THAT GIRL-- UNBELIEVABLE! A LIVING DREAM!
THE 8TH WONDER OF THE WORLD!
TIRED. SO VERY TIRED.
I'VE GOT TO REST.
IF I COULD-- LIE DOWN...
HOLL
JUST FOR--A --MINUTE...

MORNING...
I'M MYSELF AGAIN.
BUT WHERE AM--? OH, I REMEMBER. LOS ANGELES.
BUT WHAT DO I DO NOW?
I'M A STRANGER IN A STRANGE CITY.
NO FAMILY, NO MONEY, NO JOB.
I KNOW IT WASN'T A DREAM. I'VE STILL GOT THE BRACELET.
BUT I CAN'T KEEP CHANGING INTO A GODDESS WITHOUT GOOD REASON.
ANYWAY, I'M LUCKY THAT ENGLISH WAS A REQUIRED SUBJECT BACK HOME.
IF I HAVE TO BE A STRANGER SOMEWHERE, L.A. ISN'T TOO BAD A CHOICE.
GREAT WEATHER. GLAMOROUS PEOPLE.
NOT A BAD PLACE FOR GODDESS-ING.
AND I'LL NEVER LACK FOR GOSSIP NEWS.
THIS IS THE HOME OF THE "NATIONAL EXPOSER."
Uh-oh. THAT GIVES ME AN IDEA.
NATIONAL E

MR. WILLARD, DO YOU WANT TO SEE ANY MORE APPLICANTS FOR THE JOB OF YOUR ASSISTANT?
NOT TODAY, CONNIE. I'VE INTERVIEWED DOZENS ALREADY.
EACH ONE WAS WORSE THAN THE LAST.
BESIDES, ALL I CAN THINK OF IS THAT INCREDIBLE FLYING FEMALE I SAW YESTERDAY.
BUT THERE'S JUST ONE MORE GIRL OUTSIDE...
OKAY, OKAY... SEND HER IN. I'LL GET RID OF HER FAST.
NATIONAL EXPOSER
NATIONAL EXPOSER
MR. WILLARD, I READ YOUR ARTICLE ABOUT THE GIRL YOU CALL "WONDER WOMAN."
YOU WROTE THAT MOST PEOPLE DON'T BELIEVE IN HER.
I WANTED YOU TO KNOW --I DO.
SHE'S GORGEOUS!
NEVER MIND WONDER WOMAN. JUST TELL ME SOMETHING...
CAN YOU READ AND WRITE?
OF COURSE.
YOU'RE HIRED!

WELL, THAT'S OKAY WITH ME.
THE LONGER IT TAKES, THE LONGER WE'LL BE TOGETHER.
SO, MY JOB IS TO HELP THE MOST ATTRACTIVE MAN I'VE EVER MET FIND-- MYSELF!
BUT I'VE GOT TO MAKE SURE WE DON'T SUCCEED.
OH, FOR THE LIFE OF A WORKING GIRL / GODDESS!

The End

# ON THE STREET...

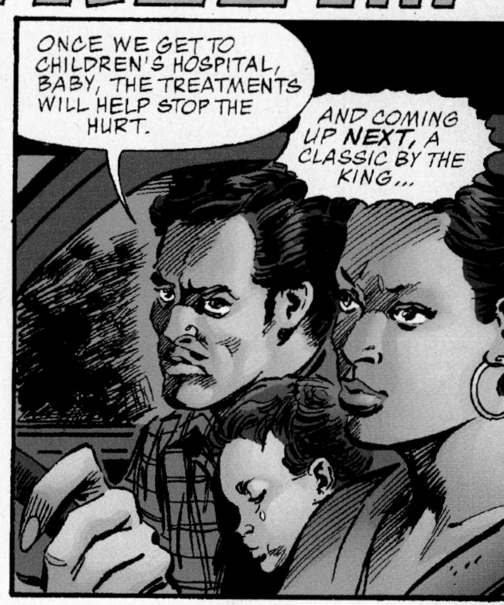

THE INNER CITY...
WHAT'S GOIN' ON OUT THERE? SOUNDS LIKE A BLASTED EARTHQUAKE!
CAN'T SEE NOTHIN' BUT SMOKE AN' DUST!
NO PARKING
FORGET IT! WE GOT BUSINESS T' DO!
BACK OFF, MAN... LEMME GO! I SWEAR I GAVE YOU ALL THE MONEY FROM THE "H" I SOLD!
YOU'RE LYIN'! AND NO EARTHQUAKE'S GONNA SAVE YOUR BUTT!
WHAT'S THAT?!
THAT LIGHT! AND THAT VOICE! DID YOU GUYS HEAR HER VOICE? IT WAS, LIKE, INSIDE MY HEAD...
YOU CAN GO, MAN. I DON' WANNA HURT YA...
I NEVER WANNA HURT ANYONE AGAIN.
WHOEVER--WHATEVER--YOU ARE... THANK YOU! THANK YOU!

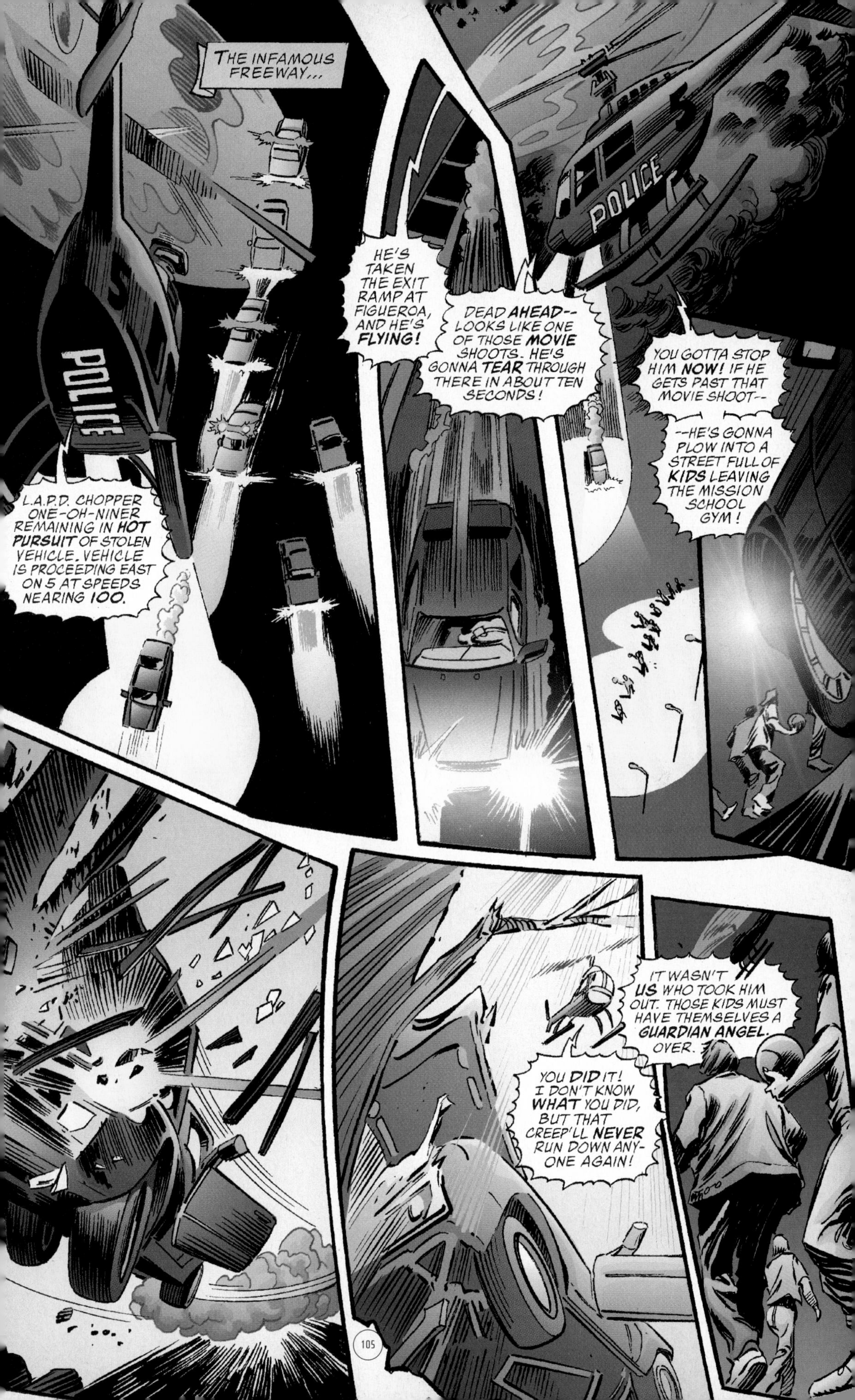
THE INFAMOUS FREEWAY...
L.A.P.D. CHOPPER ONE-OH-NINER REMAINING IN HOT PURSUIT OF STOLEN VEHICLE. VEHICLE IS PROCEEDING EAST ON 5 AT SPEEDS NEARING 100.
POLICE
5
HE'S TAKEN THE EXIT RAMP AT FIGUEROA, AND HE'S FLYING!
DEAD AHEAD-- LOOKS LIKE ONE OF THOSE MOVIE SHOOTS. HE'S GONNA TEAR THROUGH THERE IN ABOUT TEN SECONDS!
POLICE
YOU GOTTA STOP HIM NOW! IF HE GETS PAST THAT MOVIE SHOOT--
--HE'S GONNA PLOW INTO A STREET FULL OF KIDS LEAVING THE MISSION SCHOOL GYM!
IT WASN'T US WHO TOOK HIM OUT. THOSE KIDS MUST HAVE THEMSELVES A GUARDIAN ANGEL. OVER.
YOU DID IT! I DON'T KNOW WHAT YOU DID, BUT THAT CREEP'LL NEVER RUN DOWN ANY-ONE AGAIN!

NEARBY...
THERE IS NO PLACE FOR THE WEAK AND THE HUMBLE... POWER ALONE CAN PREVAIL. FOR POWER IS ALL!
Church of Eternal Empowerment
REVEREND
I OFFER YOU THE POWER OF DARKNESS... FOR LIGHT CANNOT STAND THE DARK.
SUDDENLY...
LOOK! UP ABOVE!
SOME KIND OF DEMON AND-- AND--
WHY AM I HERE? WHY WAS I LISTENING TO DARRK?
--AND THAT LIGHT!
I FEEL AS THOUGH A VEIL HAS BEEN LIFTED...
HOME. HAVE TO GO HOME.
I'VE ABSORBED SUCH POWER!
RUN! ALL OF YOU! I CAN SUMMON YOU AGAIN AT ANY TIME! NONE CAN ESCAPE ME NOW!
DARKNESS SHALL YET PREVAIL!

AND HIGH ON THE SIGNPOST FRAMING THE CITY OF BROKEN DREAMS...
CAN'T STAND IT ANYMORE. NOT SLEEPING... THE PILLS... THE DRINKS... THE PRESSURES. NO MORE.
I'M SORRY... SO SORRY... MOM, DAD, LUIS... MY POOR LUIS...
WHAT LIGHT IS THIS?
I FEEL TIRED. SO VERY TIRED.
I'VE GOT TO REST... IF I COULD LIE DOWN ... JUST FOR... A MINUTE.
DAWN...
I FEEL WHOLE AGAIN. LUIS! HE NEEDS ME. MUST CLIMB DOWN... GET HOME.
THAT LIGHT. A DREAM? A MIRACLE?
I WONDER...

THE MUSEUM SITS ATOP A HILL...
SPECIAL DELIVERY... FROM PERU, NO LESS... FOR DIANA PRINCE.
I'M DIANA PRINCE.
SIGN HERE.
GREAT TO MEET YOU, MS. PRINCE. I READ ABOUT YOU IN THE "SUNDAY TIMES" AND SAW YOU ON THAT DIS-COVERY CHANNEL SPECIAL.
THANK YOU. BEING CURATOR OF SUCH A RENOWNED MUSEUM SOMETIMES GIVES ME MORE PUBLICITY THAN I DESIRE.
POSTAL SERVICE
THAT WHAT I THINK IT IS?
DOUBT IT. I NEVER GOT A CALL FROM STEVE TREVOR ABOUT A NEW PURCHASE FROM CUZCO.
COME ON, DIANA! THIS COULD BE BIG! I MAY ONLY BE YOUR ASSISTANT, BUT IF YOU DON'T OPEN THAT, I WILL!
RELAX, CARTER. I'M AS CURIOUS AS YOU.
STRANGE! NO NOTE FROM STEVE, BUT IT HAS TO BE FROM THE DIG IN CUZCO AND--! CARTER!
WOW!
WHAT'S THAT?!?

TWO ANCIENT RUNES FROM THE INCAN CITY.
THEY WERE BELIEVED TO CONTAIN THE POWERS OF VARIOUS DEMONS.
TREVOR'S BEEN SENDING US TREASURES FROM GUITEZ FOR MONTHS. BUT THESE LOOK SPECIAL!
BUT THERE ARE SO MANY INCAN LEGENDS AND PROPHECIES CONCERNING RUNES! HOW DO WE I.D. THESE?
LOOK AT THE MARKINGS! THE HEAD OF A HAWK-MAN AND A HAWK-WOMAN!
I KNOW FROM ALL MY RESEARCH-- THESE TWO WERE WORSHIPPED AS THE MOST POWERFUL RUNES OF ALL!
WHAT DO WE DO? E-MAIL TREVOR FOR AN EXPLANATION?
IF WE HAVEN'T HEARD FROM STEVE ABOUT THESE YET... WE MAY NEVER HEAR FROM HIM.

SAUNDERS?
I THINK STEVE TREVOR'S IN BIG TROUBLE IN CUZCO. GET OUR PERUVIAN SECURITY TEAM THERE PRONTO!
WHAT NOW?
WE WAIT.
SO, BOSS... WHAT'S THE STORY OF THOSE TWO HAWK-LIKE RUNES?
LEGEND SAYS INCAN DEMONS WERE IMPRISONED WITHIN ANCIENT RUNES BY MANCO CAPAC, THE SUN GOD.
BY SMASHING A RUNE, A HUMAN COULD FREE THE DEMON AND INSTANTLY ABSORB ITS MYSTIC POWER.
AND YOU BELIEVE THAT? YOU THINK YOU AND I WOULD MORPH INTO SOME OMNIPOTENT HAWK-WOMAN AND HAWK-MAN IF WE DROPPED THESE NOW?
DO YOU, CARTER?
IT'S NONSENSE ...ANCIENT SUPERSTITION!
PERHAPS... BUT I NOTICE YOU'RE NOT DROPPING THEM.
End

Fade in: Little Asian kid drawing doodles of super-hero characters. Scattered Marvel comic books strewn around him as he draws literally on his hands and knees as kids are wont to do. He looks up in sheer shock as cosmic Kirby crackle fills the scene. Out steps a glowing being of pure white energy.

Being of Light (booming voice): "Greetings Earthling Jim, I am the Predictor. I am here to tell you that someday, you will become a comic book artist."

Earthling Jim looks back down and keeps drawing.

Earthling Jim: "Uh-huh... sure..."

Being of Light looks disappointed at Jim's nonchalance and grumbles. The intensity of crackle is now electrifying!

Being of Light: "Someday you will get to work with The Man... Stan Lee!"

Earthling Jim picks up a well-worn Marvel comic Stan wrote, stares at the credits... finally looks up looking a little more awed.

Earthling Jim: "Whoa." (pause) "Think I should change my name so people don't think we're related?"

Being of Light is clearly disappointed that he is not making much of an impression on the kid.

Being of Light: "Someday, not only will you be a comic book artist who will get to work with the man... Stan Lee — but you will do it... at DC Comics!"

Earthling Jim is clearly stunned!

Earthling Jim (scornfully): "Yeah, right..." Tosses comic book at Being of Light which bounces off the Predictor's head. Head pops off, revealing the face of someone who looks a lot like DC Executive Editor Mike Carlin.

Mike Carlin look-alike grabs the kid by the shoulders and kneels down to look him in the eye.

Mike Carlin look-alike says in a normal, but slightly annoyed voice: "Look kid, I didn't come all the way into the past to waste my time. Here's the plot to "Just Imagine if Stan Lee created Wonder Woman." Get crackin' now... yer barely gonna make the deadline as it is..."

Mike Carlin look-alike half smiles as he fades away...

Li'l kid silently nods his head as we fade to black, the frame of the shot shrinking and spinning in circles faster and faster as the sound of a clicking clock grows louder and louder.

Earthling Jim: "Waaiiiitt... what's my page raaaaate..." (voice trails off).

Okay, it didn't quite happen like that, but it was a dream come true to get to work with Stan. As a kid growing up on Marvel comics and the tales of the Marvel Bullpen, I knew of the so-called "Marvel" style of working pioneered by creative honcho Stan "The Man" Lee, visionary Jack "The King" Kirby and numerous other talented creators. The one where the artist drew a story based on a loose plot or even a conversation with the writer. After the art was complete, the writer would come back in and script the dialogue, enhancing and bringing to life the stories which had been drawn. It was the type of close collaboration a young kid could easily romanticize and daydream about.
And I did.

So just imagine how incredible it was to get to work with Stan Lee. While we didn't work in a Bullpen, we did communicate by fax and phone, and it was a real treat which is not only a tremendous career highlight but like I said, a dream come true. Thanks, Stan.

**— Jim Lee**

AH!

The BEGINNING...
A FAR DISTANT GALAXY IN ANOTHER UNIVERSE.
NO POINT TELLING YOU ITS NAME.
YOU COULDN'T EVEN BEGIN TO PRONOUNCE IT.
JUST THINK, SALDEN, THE DISCOVERY OF THE SPACE/TIME BENDER WILL CHANGE OUR WORLD FOREVER.
WE'LL BE ABLE TO REACH OTHER GALAXIES IN THE WINK OF AN EYE.
ALL BECAUSE OF THAT NEW, GREEN ELEMENT THAT ALLOWS A SPACESHIP TO BEND BOTH SPACE AND TIME!
ISN'T IT THE MOST EXCITING THING YOU CAN IMAGINE?
I GET ENOUGH KICKS WORKING AS A LAW BRINGER, LYELLA.
AND WHEN I'M BACK FROM MOPPING UP THE SLIMEBALLS, THEN YOU, BABY, PROVIDE ALL THE EXCITEMENT I NEED.
NOTE: I'VE TAKEN THE LIBERTY OF TRANSLATING OUR CHARACTERS' DIALOGUE INTO BASIC EARTH, FOR THOSE OF YOU WHOSE GALACTIC VOCABULARY MAY BE A BIT RUSTY.
— STRAIGHT-TALKIN' STAN

IF ONLY YOU DIDN'T SPEND SO MUCH TIME ON THAT MUSCLE-BUILDING DEVICE.
TO ME YOU'RE PERFECT AS YOU ARE.
I THANK YOU FOR THAT, HONEY--
--BUT YOU KNOW THE REASON I DO WHAT I DO.
HAVE YOU FORGOTTEN THE OTHER LAW BRINGERS IN MY SQUAD?
I ONLY REMEMBER HOW MUCH I LOVE YOU.

AND YOU ARE LIFE ITSELF TO ME.
BUT THE OTHERS HAVE BEEN GENETICALLY ALTERED!
THEY'RE ALL BIGGER AND STRONGER THAN ME.
YOU KNOW I CAN'T BEAR BEING THE WEAKEST OF ALL.
I WANT TO BE THE MIGHTIEST, THE BEST.
I WANT MY EXPLOITS TO BE AS STRONG AS MY LOVE FOR YOU.
NOW IT'S TIME TO JOIN THE SQUAD.
I WISH YOU DIDN'T HAVE TO GO, DARLING.
I HAVE A STRANGE SENSE OF IMPENDING DOOM!

DON'T WORRY, LYELLA...
NOT ALL THE HOUNDS OF HELL WILL STOP ME FROM RETURNING TO YOU.
I KNOW YOU MEAN THAT, MY LOVE...

BUT WHY DO I HAVE THIS FEELING THAT I'LL NEVER SEE YOU AGAIN?

THIS NEW SHOULDER HARNESS THE DEPARTMENT ISSUED ME IS THE QUIETEST OF ALL.
EVEN AT FULL POWER, IT DOESN'T MAKE A SOUND.
SILENT FLYING HARNESSES, SPACE-TIME BENDERS-- THERE'S NOTHING SCIENCE CAN'T DO!
DOWN BELOW-- MY SQUAD'S ALREADY IN ACTION.
I'M JUST IN TIME.

STAY BEHIND US, SALDEN. WE'LL TAKE FIRST IMPACT.
HEY, I MAY BE THE SMALLEST, BUT NOBODY DOES MY FIGHTING FOR ME !
DON'T BE A FOOL. WE'RE GENETICALLY ALTERED, REMEMBER?
YOU'LL ONLY GET IN THE WAY, LITTLE MAN.

BEFORE ANOTHER BREATH CAN BE DRAWN...
LOOK OUT!
THEY GOT STUN BOMBS!
THEY'RE GONNA-- unnghh

IT'S UP TO ME NOW!
STILL SECONDS TILL THIS BOMB GOES OFF!
THAT'S ALL THE TIME I NEED!

NOW YOU STAY BACK, SQUADMEN, WHILE I SAVE YOUR BUTTS!
I'LL TOSS THE BOMB OVER THE CRUISER--TO THE STARBOARD SIDE--
--THAT'LL MAKE THEM DIRECT THEIR FIRE AWAY FROM US!

HEY! SOMEONE'S ATTACKING FROM THE OTHER SIDE!
SO WHAT? YOU GOT A BLASTER-- USE IT!

WHILE THEY'RE LOOKING THE OTHER WAY, I'LL GET IN THROUGH THIS HATCH!
THE SQUADMEN WOULDA BEEN TOO BIG TO FIT.

THE HOSTAGES ARE SAFE!
AND THERE'S ONLY A HANDFUL OF CREEPS!
HEY, SPACE SCUM! TURN AROUND!

FIGURED THAT WOULD GET YOUR ATTENTION.
GREAT! I SPUN YOU AROUND JUST ENOUGH--
--FOR YOU TO BLAST YOUR PUG-UGLY PARTNER!

THAT POLISHES OFF THOSE TWO, AND--
HEY, WAIT YOUR TURN!

THIS'LL SHUT YA UP, SQUAD SLIME!
NOT WITH **THAT** AIM, IT WON'T!
WANNA KNOW HOW TO REALLY SHUT SOMEONE UP?
TRY SOMETHING--
--LIKE **THIS**!

LATER, AT THE PRECINCT...
--IN TONIGHT'S HOLOGRAM NEWS, ANOTHER TERRORIST ATTACK WAS FOILED--
GOOD WORK, SQUADMAN SALDEN!
THANKS, CAPTAIN.
I'LL BE HEADING HOME NOW.
IN A MAX-SECURITY PRISON YARD...
GET 'IM, GORROK!
NOBODY RATS ON GORROK! NOBODY!
FREEZE, CONVICT! THAT'S AN ORDER!
NO, GORROK! DON'T! PLEASE--!
I WARNED YOU, GORROK!
AS THE GUARD FIRES...
unnhhh!
YOU WANNA BLAST SOMEONE?
BLAST HIM!
NO PRISON CAN HOLD GUNDOR GORROK!
GIMME THAT FLYIN' HARNESS!
YOU'RE LUCKY I'M IN A HURRY...
SO MAYBE I'LL LETCHA LIVE.
NOW, I GOT OTHER FISH TO FRY.
IT'S PAYBACK TIME FOR THE CREEP WHO SENT ME HERE!

SALDEN SHOULD BE HOME ANY MINUTE NOW.
IF ONLY I COULD SHAKE THIS AWFUL FEELING OF DANGER, OF IMPENDING DISASTER.
OH, GOOD. I THINK I HEAR HIM AT THE DOOR NOW.

WHERE IS HE??
WHERE'S THAT ROTTEN, LOUSY BADGE-TOTER WHO HAD ME SENT AWAY?!
HE'S NOT HERE!
BUT HE'LL SEND YOU BACK AGAIN-- FOR GOOD-- WHEN HE COMES!

SECONDS LATER...
YOU GOT A FRONT ROW SEAT...
...TO SEE WHAT I DO TO 'IM WHEN HE GETS HERE!

SIRENS!
THE BLASTED SQUAD-MEN MUSTA TRACED ME TO HERE!
BUT I'LL GET MY REVENGE EVEN IF I CAN'T WAIT FOR SALDEN!

NO SOONER HAS GORROK LEFT, WHEN...
LYELLA! LYELLA!
NOOOOO
Something to remember me by!
Gorrok

LYELLA IS DEAD!
GORROK KILLED HER BECAUSE OF ME!
I'VE LOST THE ONE WHO MEANT MORE TO ME THAN ANYTHING ELSE IN THE WORLD!

WHAT STARTS AS ANGUISH TURNS INTO SEARING, BLAZING, WHITE-HOT RAGE!
WHERE IS HE? WHERE'S GORROK? TALK, OR I'LL--
SIMMER DOWN, SQUAD-MAN. HE'S HEADED FOR THE LAUNCH PAD WHERE THEY'RE TESTIN' THE SPACE/TIME BENDER!
WE'RE ARMING UP TO GO AFTER HIM.
ARMING UP???
I'LL TEAR HIM APART WITH MY BARE HANDS!

AT THE LAUNCH PAD...
THERE'S NO PLACE IN THIS GALAXY LEFT FOR ME TO HIDE!
BUT THAT AIN'T STOPPIN' GUNDOR GORROK!
THIS TWO-MAN SPACE/TIME BENDER IS MY TICKET OUTTA HERE!

AND SINCE IT'S THE ONLY SHIP OF ITS KIND--
--THERE'S NO OTHERS THAT CAN FOLLOW ME!
SO ONCE I SET COURSE FOR AN AIR-BREATHIN' PLANET IN ANOTHER GALAXY, I'M HOME FREE!
TOO BAD I DIDN'T HAVE TIME TO POLISH OFF SALDEN ALSO!
BUT THAT'S THE BREAKS.

STOP THE SHIP! STOP THE SHIP!
WELL, WELL-- LOOKS LIKE I'LL STILL HAVE MY CHANCE TO TAKE CARE OF SALDEN!
HOW LUCKY CAN YA BE?!
I'LL MAKE IT EASY FOR HIM BY OPENIN' THE DOOR!
WELCOME ABOARD, CREEP! HOPE YOU SAID YOUR PRAYERS!
PRAYERS WON'T HELP YOU, GORROK! NOTHING WILL!
I'M GONNA PAY YOU BACK IN SPADES FOR WHAT YOU DID TO LYELLA!
WHEN I'M THROUGH WITH YOU, YOU'LL--
ARRGHH! WHA-WHAT'S HAPPENING?!
NOTHIN' MUCH. JUST FIGURED THIS WAS A GOOD TIME TO BLAST OFF--
--CONSIDERIN' THAT I'M BELTED IN AND YOU'RE NOT!
THWONK!

LATER...
WAKE UP, LOSER! YOU'VE GOT TWO CHOICES!
YOU WANT A FULL BLAST THAT'LL TEAR YOUR HEAD OFF?
OR DO YOU WANT HER ON LOW, SO YOU CAN SUFFER A WHILE?
HOW ABOUT A THIRD CHOICE?
HOW ABOUT I DO WHAT ALL THE PRISONS AND LOCKUPS COULDN'T DO?
HOW ABOUT I RID THE UNIVERSE OF YOU ONCE AND FOR ALL, YOU SLIMY, STINKIN', MURDERIN' MAGGOT?
AS THE SAVAGE BATTLE CONTINUES, THE PROTOTYPE SPACE SHIP TEARS ITS WAY THROUGH SPACE/TIME, ENTERING A DISTANT GALAXY IN ANOTHER PART OF THE VAST, UNENDING UNIVERSE...

YOUR FIGHT WAS WITH *ME*, YOU SPINELESS SCUM!
BUT YOU KILLED MY INNOCENT, DEFENSELESS WIFE--
--LIKE THE MISERABLE COWARD YOU ARE!
THE SHIP! IT'S CAREENING TOWARDS THE PLANET BELOW!
GOTTA SLOW IT DOWN! IT'S PLUMMETING OUT OF CONTROL!
THE INSTRUMENTS ARE NEW TO ME--NO TIME TO STUDY THEM!

I SET THE CONTROLS FOR AN OXYGEN-BASED PLANET, SO THIS'LL DO ME FINE.
WHATEVER FORM OF LIFE THEY GOT HERE, I'LL FIND A WAY TO TAKE OVER--LIKE I ALWAYS DO!
AT LEAST I'M FINALLY RID OF SALDEN!

SHIP--STILL PLUMMETING. ABOUT TO CRASH. NO TIME--TO DO ANYTHING...

WHOOOM

THE WATER CUSHIONED THE IMPACT!

BUT I'M TRAPPED--AT THE BOTTOM OF THE SEA!

THE CONTROLS ARE SMASHED --USELESS.
THERE'S NO WAY OUT!

WHAT A WAY TO END UP!
RUNNING OUT OF AIR MILES BELOW THE SURFACE OF A STRANGE PLANET IN AN UNKNOWN GALAXY!

EVEN IF I TRIED TO SWIM TO THE SURFACE, THE HATCH DOOR OPENS OUTWARD--
THERE'S NO WAY I COULD PUSH IT OUT AGAINST THE PRESSURE OF COUNTLESS TONS OF OCEAN WATER!
IF WE WERE ON LAND, IT WOULD BE SO SIMPLE...
ALL I'D HAVE TO DO IS LOOSEN THE BOLT AND PUT MY SHOULDER TO THE DOOR, LIKE THIS.

AS SALDEN LEANS AGAINST THE HEAVY DOOR, THE IMPOSSIBLE HAPPENS...
IT OPENED!!!

MILES FROM THE SURFACE--NEVER MAKE IT--BUT MIGHT AS WELL TRY!

IT--CAN'T BE! I SWAM LIKE A TORPEDO!
AND THE INDESCRIBABLE WATER PRESSURE--
--IT DIDN'T EVEN SLOW ME DOWN!

STRANGE-- THAT GREENISH GLOW SPREADING OVER THE WATER...
MUST BE THE NEW MINERAL SUBSTANCE THAT HELPED POWER THE SHIP!
WAIT! ARE MY EYES PLAYING TRICKS--OR IS THAT A CITY IN THE DISTANCE?
IT'S A LONG WAY TO GO, BUT I HAVEN'T ANY CHOICE!
IT--ISN'T POSSIBLE! I'M SWIMMING LIKE A HUMAN MISSILE!
EVEN THOSE HUNGRY, SHARP-TOOTHED SEA CREATURES CAN'T KEEP UP WITH ME!

MAYBE I'M HALLUCINATING.
I'VE GOTTA REST--SORT THINGS OUT.

MINUTES LATER...
HEY, WE FOUND OURSELVES A TURKEY!
MUSTA HAD TOO MUCH T' DRINK AT SOME SNOOTY BEACH HOUSE COSTUME PARTY.

WAKE UP, PRETTY BOY!
ANYONE SLEEPS ON OUR BEACH GOTTA PAY FOR THE PRIV'LEGE!

I DON'T UNDERSTAND YOUR STUPID-SOUNDING LINGO--
BUT NOBODY MAULS ME, GET IT?
REMEMBER, CLASS, WE'RE TRANSLATING SALDEN'S SPEECH INTO ENGLISH FOR YOU FROM ITS ORIGINAL BASIC INTER-GALACTIC! -SCHOLARLY STAN
WHA--? NO ONE CAN LIFT ME WITH ONE HAND LIKE THAT!

WE'LL MAKE MINCEMEAT OF YA FOR THAT! YOU'LL WISH YA NEVER--
YEEEOW!
I SENT THEM FLYING!
BUT HOW? I DIDN'T HIT 'EM THAT HARD!
DAMN! MY WRIST COMMUNI-CATOR FELL OFF!
BUT-- I DON'T GET IT! LOOK HOW SLOW IT'S FALLING!
LIKE IT'S ON A CUSHION OF AIR!
BACK HOME, IT WOULD'VE HIT THE GROUND IN A SPLIT SECOND.
ON THIS PLANET, I'M FAST AS A WHIRLWIND. STRONG AS--
OF COURSE! THERE'S ONLY ONE ANSWER!
IT'S GRAVITY! MY HOME WORLD'S GRAVITY IS A HUNDRED TIMES STRONGER--!
MY MUSCLES ARE USED TO STRUGGLING AGAINST A MUCH GREATER PULL!
HERE, I FEEL NO RESISTANCE-- LIKE I'M MOVING IN A VACUUM!
COMPARED TO THE PEOPLE ON THIS WORLD-- I'M SOME SORT OF SUPER MAN!
THEY PROBABLY DON'T REALIZE HOW SLOW AND PONDEROUS THEIR VEHICLES ARE.
BACK HOME, OUR SLOWEST SHOULDER HARNESS COULD OUTPACE THOSE CUMBERSOME MACHINES.
LOOKS LIKE I'LL BE STUCK HERE FOR A WHILE...
SO I'D BETTER SEE WHAT THE REST OF THEIR PRIMITIVE CIVILIZA-TION IS LIKE!

ONE THING'S FOR SURE--
WITH THIS LIGHT GRAVITY, I'LL HAVE NO TROUBLE GETTING AROUND.
EXCEPT-- I DON'T KNOW WHERE I'M GOING!

BECAUSE THE ATMOSPHERE'S SO THIN, I'VE GOT SOME KIND OF TELESCOPIC VISION!
I CAN SEE MUCH FURTHER THAN I COULD BACK HOME!

HOME! THE WORD IS MEANINGLESS NOW!
THERE'S NO WAY I'LL EVER GET BACK.
EVEN IF I **COULD** GO BACK...
LYELLA IS GONE-- FOREVER!
BUT I STILL MUST RETURN-- TO HONOR HER MEMORY!
BUT NOT UNTIL I AVENGE HER DEATH!
***GORROK!*** WHEREVER HE IS--I'LL FIND HIM!
I'LL USE MY SHOULDER HARNESS TO CRUISE THE SURFACE IN SEARCH OF--
NO! WHAT'S WRONG?
IT DOESN'T WORK!
THE CRASH MUST HAVE BROKEN ITS SENSITIVE POWER CELL!
NO MATTER!
I'LL WEAR IT ANYWAY... AS A REMINDER OF THE WORLD I'VE LOST!

S'MATTER, DUDE, DIDJA LOSE THE STARSHIP ENTERPRISE?
LISTEN TO THEM!
I'M MAROONED ON A PLANET OF CLOWNS!
THEIR LANGUAGE IS SO SIMPLE, I'VE FATHOMED IT ALREADY.*
HEY, GLOP ONTO THE FAR-OUT HUNK!
WOW! HE COULD FRAZZLE MY FANTASIES ANY TIME!
*WHICH IS LUCKY FOR ME! NO MORE TRANSLATING! -- LAZYBONES LEE

YOU CALL THIS A TEST?!?
I'LL SHOW YOU A **REAL** TEST!

I DON'T WANNA SKIN MY KNUCKLES BY BASHIN' IN YOUR SKULLS, SO--

I'LL JUST MOP YOU UP THE EASY WAY!

GREAT IS GORROK!
GORROK IS GOD!
ALL MUST DO AS GORROK COMMANDS!
YEAH, RIGHT.
GORROK'S GONNA LIKE IT HERE!

THIS IS THE LIFE.
NOT A WORRY IN THE WORLD.
LIVIN' LIKE A KING.
AND THAT LOSER, SALDEN, ROTTIN' AT THE BOTTOM OF THE SEA!
IF WE DANCE WELL FOR MIGHTY GORROK...
PERHAPS HE WILL LOOK UPON US WITH FAVOR.
BUT THE MERCILESS "GOD" SOON GROWS RESTLESS...

THERE MUST BE SOME REAL CITIES SOMEWHERE.
WHY SHOULD I RULE A PACK OF SAVAGES WHEN I COULD TAKE OVER THE WHOLE PLANET!
BRING ME TO THE NEAREST SEAPORT-- AND BE QUICK ABOUT IT!

WITH MY NEW SUPER STRENGTH, NOTHING CAN STOP ME.
I'LL TURN THIS WHOLE WORLD INTO GORROK'S EMPIRE OF SLAVES!

HOLD IT! THE TENT POLE ISN'T CENTERED RIGHT.

A SUDDEN, STUNNING SILENCE PERVADES THE BIG TOP!

THE AUDIENCE IS TOO SPELLBOUND TO UTTER A SOUND!

THERE! THAT'S BETTER

AND NOW THAT I HAVE EVERYONE'S ATTENTION-

I'LL START MY TRAPEZE ACT!

NO NEED TO CLIMB THE LADDER.
IT'LL TAKE TOO LONG.
ESPECIALLY WHEN I CAN JUMP TO THE TOP OF THE TENT.
WOW! DID YOU SEE THAT?!
HOW DID HE DO IT?
BETCHA HE'S GOT SPECIAL SPRINGS INSIDE HIS BOOTS!
LOOK WHAT HE'S DOING NOW!
ARE YOU SURE YOU CAN KEEP THIS UP?
LADY, YOU HAVEN'T SEEN ANYTHING YET!
WHERE'S THE GUINNESS BOOK OF RECORDS WHEN WE NEED IT?
FOR THE NEXT HALF-HOUR, SALDEN USES ALL HIS NEWLY ACQUIRED SUPER ABILITY TO DAZZLE THE AUDIENCE AND THE PERFORMERS ALIKE...
WE'D SHOW YOU MORE OF HIS ACT, BUT KNOWING HOW HIP OUR READERS ARE, WE FIGURE YOU GET THE IDEA.

OKAY, CLARK. YOU'RE HIRED. YOU CAN START TOMORROW.
I'LL BUILD OUR WHOLE SHOW AROUND YOU--MAKE YOU A STAR!
FORGET IT. THAT'S KID STUFF.
I JUST NEEDED A STAKE TO TIDE ME OVER.
THERE'S SOMETHING IMPORTANT I'VE GOTTA DO.

LATER...*
I MADE ENOUGH MONEY TO RENT THIS DUMP AND BUY A COMPUTER AND A TV SO I CAN LEARN MORE ABOUT THIS CRUMMY PLANET.
BUT I DON'T LIKE WHAT I'M LEARNING.
* MY FAVORITE KIND OF CAPTION. DOESN'T REQUIRE MUCH EFFORT TO THINK IT UP! -- ENERGY-SAVIN' STAN

THEY'VE ONLY TAKEN THE FIRST STEPS IN SPACE TRAVEL.
THEY'RE NOWHERE NEAR DISCOVERING THE SPACE/TIME BENDER.
THAT MEANS I'M STUCK HERE! MY CHANCES OF RETURNING ARE NIL!

BUT THEY HAVE ALL THE BASIC KNOWLEDGE.
WHY IS THEIR SPACE PROGRESS SO SLOW?
FROM WHAT I SEE ON TV, IT'S BECAUSE MOST OF THEIR MONEY IS WASTED.
IT'S SPENT ON FIGHTING CRIME, ARMING FOR WAR AND FIGHTING TERRORISM.

BUT MAYBE FATE SENT ME HERE FOR A REASON. MAYBE I CAN MAKE A DIFFERENCE.
IF MY POWERS COULD HELP ABOLISH WAR AND CRIME, MAYBE THEY'D HAVE THE TRILLIONS THEY'LL NEED TO SPAN THE GALAXIES!

AND THEN, WITH THE COSMOS NO LONGER DENIED THEM...
I COULD RETURN, TO HONOR THE MEMORY OF THE WOMAN I'VE LOVED!
BRINNG
THE DOORBELL?

YOU'RE THE MAN FROM THE CIRCUS.
IT WAS DIFFICULT FINDING YOU.
MY NEWSPAPER WOULD LIKE TO KNOW...
HANG YOUR PAPER! I'M BUSY. GET LOST.

NO TIME FOR INTERVIEWS. FIRST, I'VE GOTTA FIND GORROK...
THEN I'LL LICK THE CRIME PROBLEM HERE--SO THEY CAN CONCENTRATE ON THEIR SPACE PROGRAM.

LOOKS LIKE THE LAST TENANT LEFT SOME COMIC BOOKS BEHIND.
HE'S GOT GOOD TASTE. THEY'RE ALL ABOUT SUPER-HEROES!

Hmmm... MOST OF 'EM TRY TO KEEP THEIR IDENTITY SECRET.
ACCORDING TO THIS, IF PEOPLE KNOW YOU'VE GOT A SUPER POWER, THEY NEVER STOP HOUNDING YOU.
THEY WANNA TURN YOU INTO A SPECIMEN--TO SEE WHAT MAKES YOU TICK!
I DIDN'T THINK OF THAT.
FURIOUS COMICS

THAT SETTLES IT.
NO ONE MUST KNOW I'M FROM A DIFFERENT PLANET.
NO ONE'S GONNA POKE AND PROBE AND TRY TO DISSECT ME!
I'LL CLAIM MY POWER COMES FROM MY SUIT!
I'LL SAY IT'S A PATENTED INVENTION OF MINE--PERIOD!
LET 'EM LIKE IT OR LUMP IT!

AT THAT MOMENT, GUNDOR GORROK HAS REACHED LOS ANGELES...
COMPARED TO ME, EVERYONE HERE IS A HELPLESS WEAKLING.
AND THAT'S HOW I LIKE IT!

JUST WHAT I NEED. AN OLD-FASHIONED MONEY MACHINE.
BACK HOME THEY STOPPED USIN' THEM YEARS AGO...

--'CAUSE THEY WERE TOO EASY TO SMASH!

MONEY LOOKS GOOD ON ANY PLANET.
NICE OF 'EM TO PROVIDE IT FOR ME.

STEALIN' MONEY IS GONNA BE TOO EASY FOR ME HERE.
I GOTTA THINK OF A WAY TO TAKE OVER THE WHOLE CITY.
JUST FOR STARTERS, OF COURSE.
Church of Eternal Empowerment Reverend dominic darrk

YOU THERE, SIR! YOU'RE JUST IN TIME!
YES, WE'VE BEEN WAITING FOR YOU.
DO COME IN.
Huh?

WHADDAYA MEAN YOU WERE WAITING FOR ME?
REVEREND DOMINIC DARRK SAID YOU WOULD BE HERE.
AND, OF COURSE, THE REVEREND IS NEVER WRONG.
YEAH? LEMME SEE THIS REVEREND OF YOURS!

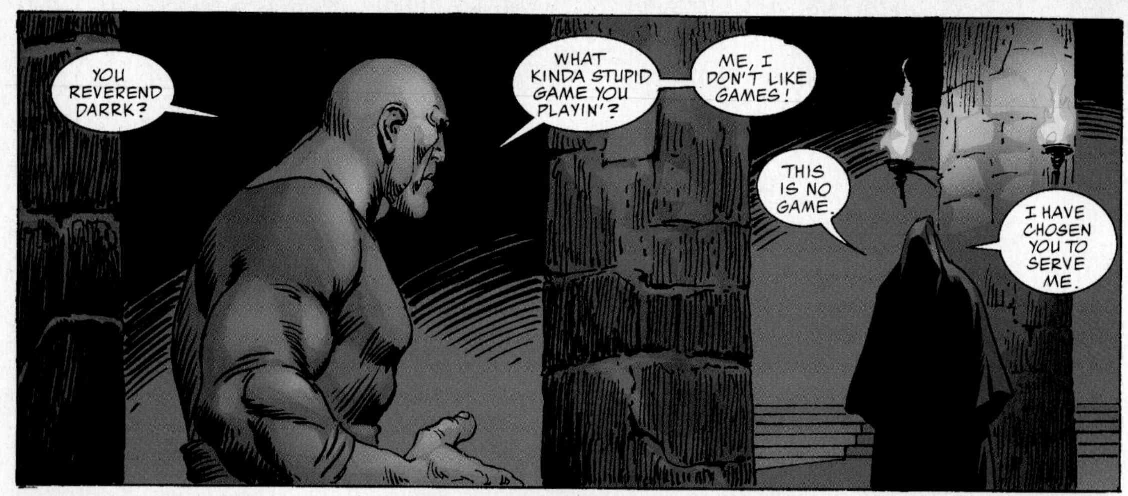

SERVE *YOU?!!*

GUNDOR GORROK SERVES NOBODY!

I'M THE STRONGEST THERE IS! I CAN DO ANYTHING!

I'LL WRAP THIS BENCH AROUND YOUR SCRAWNY NECK!

THERE IS MORE TO POWER THAN BRUTE STRENGTH!

WITH THE MEREST THOUGHT--

--I TURN YOUR BENCH TO ASHES!

HEL-LOOO, MR. KENT.

MY NAME IS **LOIS LANE**. I HEARD ABOUT YOUR CIRCUS ACT.

CONGRATULATIONS, BUT I'M BUSY. GOODBYE.

DON'T YOU WANT TO HEAR MY OFFER?

NO.

I SEE THAT YOU'RE THE SHY TYPE.

I LIKE THAT IN A MAN.

I'M AN AGENT. I CAN MAKE YOU RICH AND FAMOUS.

IF I BECOME FAMOUS, GORROK MAY COME AFTER ME!

COME IN, MISS LANE.

I'VE A GREAT PUBLICITY GIMMICK FOR YOU.

WE'LL CALL YOU "SUPERMAN." IT'LL GO OVER GREAT WITH THE PUBLIC.

PEOPLE WILL PAY A FORTUNE TO SEE YOU PERFORM YOUR AMAZING FEATS.

AND THINK OF THE TOYS, GAMES, T-SHIRTS...!

AS LONG AS IT BRINGS GORROK OUT OF HIDING!

NO TELLING HOW LONG IT WOULD TAKE ME TO FIND GORROK.
BUT IF SHE CAN DO WHAT SHE SAYS, IT'S SURE TO BRING HIM TO ME.
I'VE GOT TO GO ALONG WITH HER.
YOU'LL BE A BIG HIT WITH THE LADIES, CLARK.
MAY I CALL YOU "CLARK"?
Huh? OH, YEAH. IT'S MY NAME, RIGHT?

PEOPLE IN THE HALL, RUSHING TOWARDS THE DOOR!
YOU'RE TOO TENSE, CLARK I DON'T HEAR ANYTHING.
THAT'S BECAUSE YOU'RE FROM EARTH.
NOBODY MOVE!
WHERE'S CLARK KENT?
FREEZE! EVERYBODY FREEZE!
YOU! IN THE COMIC BOOK SUIT! STAY WHERE YOU ARE!

RELAX. I WASN'T GOING ANYWHERE.
LUCKY FOR YOU, MISTER! WE'RE GOVERNMENT AGENTS!
WE'RE HERE FOR YOUR SUIT!

OH, IS THAT ALL?
HERE, TAKE IT. I'D LIKE IT DRY CLEANED AND RETURNED IN THE MORNING. NO STARCH, OKAY?
DON'T BE FUNNY. IT'S GOIN' TO THE PENTAGON TO BE TESTED.
TESTED? YOU DIDN'T EVEN GIVE IT TIME TO STUDY.
WATCH YOUR LIP, MISTER. WE'RE GOVERNMENT!

THIS SHOULDER HARNESS IS WHAT LETS YOU JUMP HIGH AND DO THOSE TRICKS, RIGHT?
RIGHT.
I'LL JUST CHECK IT OUT MYSELF WHILE I'M HERE.

SO OKAY, I'LL JUST TAKE A JUMP AND LET THE GIZMO DO THE REST.
HERE GOES!
CAREFUL, SAM.

UMPHHH!
MAYBE THERE'S A TRICK TO IT.

AWRIGHT, WISE GUY, WHAT'S THE ANSWER?
HOW D'YA MAKE IT WORK?
THAT'S MY SECRET.
I'M COUNTIN' ON IT TO MAKE ME RICH.
BUT ONCE THE SECRET'S OUT, I'M JUST ANOTHER NOWHERE GUY.

HOLD EVERY-THING!
CLARK KENT IS MY CLIENT!
I'VE GOT ALL KINDSA WRITS!

YOU CAN'T LEGALLY TAKE THAT SHOULDER HARNESS!
RETURN IT OR WE SUE!
OKAY, OKAY. KEEP YOUR SHIRT ON.

THANKS FOR YOUR HELP, MISTER, BUT HOW'D YOU GET HERE?
I HIRED HIM FOR YOU.
WHEN LOIS LANE IS YOUR AGENT, YOUR BUTT'S ALWAYS PROTECTED.
NOW LET'S TALK ABOUT A LARRY KING INTERVIEW.

THE TV'S STILL ON! THERE'S A NEWS FLASH!
THE CHINESE PRESIDENT WAS CAPTURED BY TERRORISTS AS HE LANDED IN LOS ANGELES ON THE FIRST LAP OF HIS TRIP TO WASHINGTON.
SOME AGITATORS CLAIM IT MIGHT BE A U.S. PLOT.
IF THE PRESIDENT ISN'T RETURNED SAFELY WITHIN 12 HOURS, IT COULD MEAN WAR!

THE TERRORISTS HAVE DEMANDED 10 BILLION DOLLARS IN A SPECIAL CONTAINER TO BE PICKED UP BY HELICOPTER.
AND THERE MUST BE NO OTHER SHIP FLYING WITHIN 500 MILES OF THAT SPOT.
IF THERE'S A WAR, IT COULD SET THEIR SPACE PROGRAM BACK FOR DECADES!
I CAN'T LET THAT HAPPEN!

YOU SET UP THE LARRY KING INTERVIEW, WHOEVER ***HE*** IS, LOIS.
I'VE GOT THINGS TO DO.

IN A WAY, I FEEL LIKE I'M ON THE POLICE SQUAD AGAIN BACK HOME.
IT'S A GOOD FEELING!

AMAZING! THOSE JETS OF HIS DON'T MAKE THE SLIGHTEST SOUND!
HOW IS THAT POSSIBLE?

THE PENTAGON...
IF WE CAN'T FIND-- AND RESCUE--THE CHINESE PRESIDENT IN THE NEXT 12 HOURS...
WE'LL HAVE TO ACCEDE TO THE TERRORISTS' DEMANDS!
THERE'S NO OTHER CHOICE!

WRONG! THERE IS A CHOICE!
I HAVE A PLAN. IT'S A LONG SHOT, BUT IT MIGHT WORK.
IT'S SOMETHING ONLY I CAN DO!
WHO IN BLUE BLAZES IS THAT?
HOW'D HE GET THROUGH THE WINDOW?
HE'S THE ONE I READ ABOUT-- FROM THE CIRCUS!
LET'S HEAR HIM OUT. HE POSSESSES UNCANNY ABILITIES!

LATER, AT THE RANSOM PICKUP SPOT...
THERE'S THE MONEY, PACKED THE WAY WE INSTRUCTED.
AND NO OTHER AIRCRAFT FOR 500 MILES.
WHEN THEY PICK UP THIS CARGO THEY'LL BE IN FOR A LITTLE SURPRISE!
BUT THERE ARE OTHER SURPRISES IN STORE...

HIGH ABOVE THE EARTH...

A U.S. SATELLITE IS IN POSITION TO TRACK THE TERRORISTS' HELICOPTER...

WITHIN SECONDS, AS IF BY A PREARRANGED SIGNAL--
--A CAVE-IN OCCURS, FILLING THE TUNNEL WITH TONS OF ROCK!
WE'RE BLOCKED!
NO WAY WE CAN FOLLOW THOSE TRACKS!

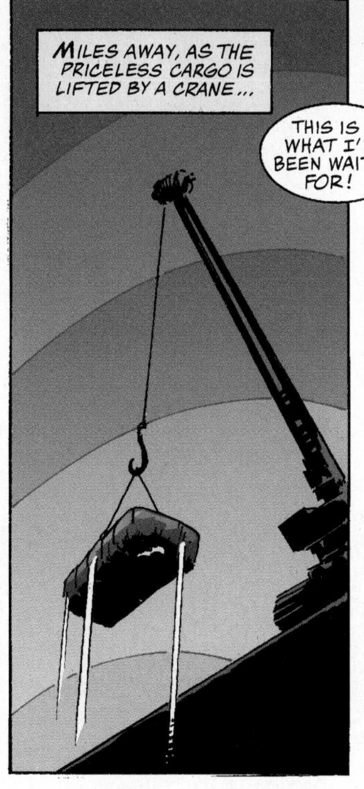
MILES AWAY, AS THE PRICELESS CARGO IS LIFTED BY A CRANE...

THIS IS WHAT I'VE BEEN WAITING FOR!
BUT ANOTHER HAS BEEN WAITING ALSO!

I HAD A HUNCH THIS LITTLE PARTY WOULD FLUSH YOU OUT!
SO I BROUGHT ALONG YOUR LADY FRIEND.
ONE FALSE MOVE AND SHE DIES!
CLARK, WHO IS THIS MAN? HOW DOES HE KNOW YOU?
GORROK! HOW'D YOU GET INVOLVED IN THIS?
IT'S A LONG STORY!

TOO BAD YOU WON'T LIVE LONG ENOUGH TO HEAR IT!
TIE 'IM UP, REAL TIGHT!

THIS IS THE END OF THE LINE FOR YOU!
YOUR KILLING DAYS ARE OVER!

BRAVE TALK FROM A MAN WITH SECONDS TO LIVE!
SAY YOUR PRAYERS, 'CAUSE THIS IS IT!

FIRST YOUR WIFE, AND NOW YOU!
AT LAST I HAVE MY FULL REVENGE FOR THE YEARS YOU MADE ME SPEND IN PRISON!
YOU SHOULDN'T HAVE SAID THAT!
YOU SHOULDN'T HAVE REMINDED ME OF LYELLA!
NOW NOTHING IN THE COSMOS CAN STOP ME!
NOTHING
NOTHI
NOTHING!!

IF YOU THINK BRUTE FORCE AND POWER ARE ALL IT TAKES--

I'LL SHOW YOU POWER SUCH AS YOU'VE NEVER KNOWN!

CLARK, YOU'RE WONDERFUL!
THIS'LL BE SURE TO GET YOU A SPOT ON JAY LENO!
AND THINK OF THE ENDORSEMENTS--NIKE! KELLOGG'S! NINTENDO!
GET REAL, LOIS! THIS ISN'T A GAME!
I'VE GOTTA GET YOU OUT OF HERE BEFORE I TACKLE GORROK AGAIN!

THERE MUST BE AN EXIT SOMEWHERE!
EVERY UNDERGROUND TUNNEL HAS A WAY OUT!
THERE! STRAIGHT AHEAD! SOMETHING ABOVE US!
HOLD ON TIGHT, LOIS!
I DON'T KNOW WHERE THIS LEADS, BUT I'VE GOTTA TRY IT!
WHAT I'D GIVE FOR A TV NEWS CREW!
THONK!
NAL BANK
FLORIST
YOU SHOULD BE SAFE HERE IN THE STREET!
I'VE GOT TO GO BACK TO FIND THE CHINESE PRESIDENT!
BUT YOU WON'T HAVE A CHANCE!
ALL THOSE MEN, THOSE GUNS!
I CAN'T LOSE THE BEST CLIENT I EVER HAD!
THAT'S THE BREAKS, LADY!
IF HE SURVIVES, I'LL SIGN HIM TO AN IRON-CLAD CON-TRACT!

OKAY, GORROK, TALK! WHERE DO I FIND YOUR HOSTAGE?

ONLY TIME'LL TELL--

AND RIGHT NOW, YOUR TIME JUST RAN OUT!

I WAS GONNA SHOOT YOU REAL FAST AND EASY BEFORE.

BUT NOW, I'M GIVIN' MY MEN A CHANCE TO MOP UP THE PLACE WITH YOU!

THEN, AFTER THEY'RE DONE, I'LL POLISH YOU OFF MYSELF!

SOME GUYS JUST NEVER LEARN!

FIRST, I'LL TAKE CARE OF YOUR STOOGES--!

NOW, GORROK, IT'S PAYOFF TIME!
GIVE ME YOUR HOSTAGE!

I'LL GIVE YA SOMETHING, ALL RIGHT--
EVEN YOUR STRENGTH WON'T SAVE YOU FROM THIS!

GOODBYE, SALDEN! YOU NEVER HAD A CHANCE AGAINST ME!
THIS CAN BORE A HOLE HALFWAY THROUGH A MOUNTAIN!

BUT IT HAS TO HIT THE MOUNTAIN FIRST!
AND I'VE GOT NEWS FOR YOU--
--YOU SHOULDN'T STAND UNDER A LANDSLIDE--

--ESPECIALLY ONE THAT YOU CAUSED YOURSELF!

THAT PUTS GORROK UNDER WRAPS!
BUT I STILL HAVEN'T FOUND THE CHINESE PRESIDENT!
AND THE 12 HOURS ARE ALMOST UP!
THE WORLD IS STILL ON THE BRINK OF WAR!

YOU MADE IT! YOU'RE SAFE!
NO ONE IS SAFE TILL WE FIND THE PRESIDENT!

IF THERE IS A WAR, THE ARMY, NAVY AND AIR FORCE WILL ALL BID FOR YOU!
AS YOUR AGENT, I'LL GET YOU THE BEST OFFER!
HOLD IT, LOIS! I JUST THOUGHT OF SOMETHING.
WHEN I ASKED WHERE TO FIND HIS HOSTAGE--
GORROK SAID, "ONLY TIME WILL TELL!"

BY THE SNEER ON HIS FACE, I GOT THE FEELING HE WAS DANGLING A CLUE IN FRONT OF ME--
A CLUE HE WAS SURE I WOULDN'T DECIPHER.
SPEAKING OF TIME, IT MIGHT STILL BE EARLY ENOUGH TO GET YOU ON THE TONIGHT SHOW.
I DROPPED MY WATCH, BUT THERE'S A CLOCK OVER THERE.

DARN! IT'S TOO FAR AWAY! I CAN'T MAKE OUT THE HANDS!

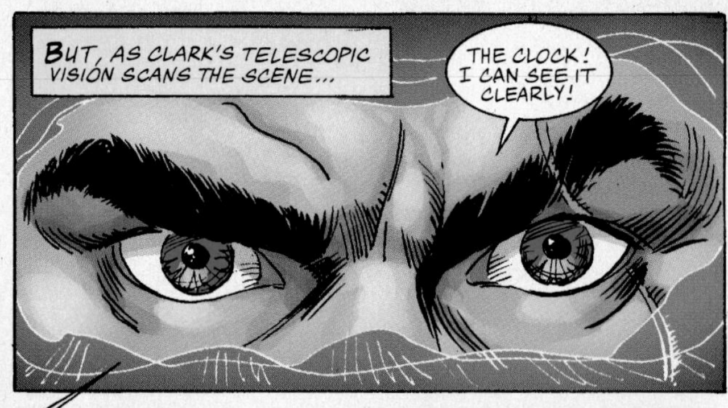
BUT, AS CLARK'S TELESCOPIC VISION SCANS THE SCENE...
THE CLOCK! I CAN SEE IT CLEARLY!

SO THAT'S WHAT GORROK MEANT!

ONLY SECONDS REMAINING!
I'VE GOTTA LEAP HIGHER THAN EVER BEFORE!

HANG IN THERE, MAN!
WE'LL MAKE IT TOGETHER!

NO LETTERED SOUND EFFECT COULD DO JUSTICE TO THIS EXPLOSION, SO WE DIDN'T BOTHER! --SCRUPULOUS STAN

HE SAVED ME! HE THREW THE BOMB HIGH INTO THE AIR!
THAT'S WHY I DUBBED HIM "SUPERMAN!"

I REALIZE YOUR GOVERNMENT WAS BLAME-LESS!
AND I AM GRATEFUL FOR THE COURAGEOUS RESCUE!
MY CLIENT IS AVAILABLE FOR OVERSEAS BOOKINGS, MR. PRESIDENT!

LATER...
YOU'RE THE TOAST OF THE MEDIA!
EVERYONE'S TALKING ABOUT SUPERMAN!
SO WHY SO GLUM, CHUM?
I'M WORRIED ABOUT GORROK! WHAT IF HE SURVIVED THAT CAVE-IN?
AND WHO HELPED HIM ASSEMBLE THAT CREW OF TERRORISTS?

HEY, IT'S OVER! FORGET ABOUT IT!
THE GOOD NEWS IS--YOU'RE GONNA BE RICHER THAN BILL GATES, MORE FAMOUS THAN BARBIE!
I'VE ALREADY HAD OFFERS FROM WARNER BROS., UNIVERSAL, DISNEY, AND THE NETWORKS ARE FALLING ALL OVER THEMSELVES!
KNOW SOMETHIN', LOIS? YOU'RE A TREAT FOR THE EYES, BUT WE'RE JUST NOT ON THE SAME WAVELENGTH!

GORROK COULDN'T HAVE PLANNED THAT HOSTAGE-TAKING BY HIMSELF!
HE HASN'T BEEN HERE LONG ENOUGH TO GET IT ALL TOGETHER.
I'LL DUMP ALL MY OTHER CLIENTS AND HANDLE CLARK EXCLUSIVELY!

AND WHY WOULD GORROK RISK CAUSING A WORLD WAR? WHAT WOULD HE HAVE TO GAIN?
I'LL COLLECT 10% AS HIS AGENT AND ANOTHER 10% AS HIS MANAGER.

I GET THE FEELING THERE'S SOMEONE ELSE INVOLVED, SOMEONE FAR MORE DANGEROUS--FAR MORE POWERFUL!
MY BIGGEST PROBLEM WILL BE KEEPING OTHER GIRLS AWAY, BUT I'M PRETTY GOOD AT THAT!

I'VE GOT TO FIND THE ONE PULLING THE STRINGS!
BUT HOW DO I START? WHERE DO I LOOK?
Church of Eternal Empowerment
REVEREND DOMINIC DARRK
The End?--YEAH, RIGHT!

# ON THE STREET

MY COUSIN'S HUSBAND STARTED THIS COMPANY IN '39!
HERE HE GOES AGAIN...

BILL GAINES HAD "MAD" COMICS. WE WENT ONE BETTER WITH "FURIOUS" COMICS!
THE "PEP" COMICS BOYS, MORRY, LOU AND JOHN, PUBLISHED "BLUE RIBBON" COMICS! WE OUT-SOLD 'EM WITH "GOLD MEDAL" COMICS! RIGHT, MIDGE?
RIGHT, JOE.

DONENFELD AND LIEBOWITZ HIT BIG WITH "WORLD'S FAIR" COMICS. I CRUSHED 'EM WITH "WORLD'S SERIES" COMICS.
...UNTIL WE GOT THAT CEASE AND DESIST LETTER FROM THE BASEBALL COMMISSIONER...
WHATEVER.

NOW, OUR SHIP'S COME IN! WE GOT US A REAL HONEST-TO-GOODNESS SUPER-HERO FROM ANOTHER PLANET. I THINK PLUTO.
MIDGE-- THROW TOGETHER AN ASH-CAN COMIC BOOK. CALL IT "PLUTO" COMICS.
Daily Planet
SUPERMAN: STRANGE VISITOR FROM ANOTHER PLANET
FORGET IT, JOE... DISNEY?

HEY... WE DON'T MESS WITH DISNEY LAWYERS.
I DON'T CARE HOW YOU DO IT... BUT GET ME SUPERMAN'S SIGNATURE ON A CONTRACT FOR COMIC BOOKS!
NOW GO! GO!

LESTER, ARE YOU MY LAWYER OR ARE YOU NOT?
UH, SURE, JOE... BUT I'M ALSO YOUR BROTHER-IN-LAW!
sigh I KNOW.

GET ON THE BALL HERE, LESTER! IF THIS SUPERMAN'S AN ALIEN, HE AIN'T PROTECTED BY THE U.S. CONSTITUTION OR ANY HUMAN BEING LAWS, IS HE?
UH, I GUESS NOT.

GUESS?! I DON'T PAY YOU TO GUESS! I PAY YOU TO KNOW! IF THERE'S NO LAW TO STOP US, WE'RE GONNA PUBLISH "SUPERMAN" COMICS WITHOUT HIS SIGNATURE!

THIS COULD BE THE BIG TIME FOR ME AT LAST, MIDGE! HERE'S WHERE "FLY BY NIGHT COMICS" FINALLY MOVES PAST DC AND MARVEL!
WISH UNCLE MANNY COULD SEE HIS "FAT NOTHING OF A NEPHEW" NOW!
REMEMBER YOUR PROCTOLOGIST APPOINTMENT IS AT 4.

Superman's
AGENT-MANAGER
LOIS LANE
555-2587
"He gets the bad guys; I get 20%."

I'M GONNA SUE YOU FOR PUBLISHING "SUPERMAN" COMIC BOOKS!
FERGET IT. THE GUY'S AN ALIEN.
ALIENS AIN'T GOT RIGHTS.

DON'T BET ON THAT, LIVER-LIPS!

NOW I'M MAD!

YOU'RE MAD? JUST WAIT'LL--
SHADDAP! YOU GOT TEN SECONDS TO GET OUT!

ACTUALLY, THAT'S ALL THE TIME I'LL NEED.

SUPERMAN? THIS IS LOIS. ARE YOU AVAILABLE TO TAKE A MEETING... RIGHT NOW? OH, GOOD!

...THREE SECONDS... FOUR SECONDS...
RMMBLL
HOLD IT!
HOLD IT!

...FIVE SECONDS ...SIX SECONDS...
CALL HIM OFF!
CALL HIM OFF!

I'LL STOP PUBLISHING SUPERMAN!
I'LL DO ANYTHING!
ANYTHING!
OKAY, OKAY, YOU SMOOTH-TALKING CHARMER ...YOU CONVINCED ME--

--BUT YOU GOTTA PAY FOR BEING A NAUGHTY LITTLE PUBLISHER!

I'LL PAY!
I'LL PAY!
IS HE GONE?
IS HE GONE?

CAREFUL, MISS. JOE'S CHECKS SOMETIMES BOUNCE.
IF THIS BOUNCES, SO WILL HE.

DC COMICS? THIS IS LOIS LANE. I REPRESENT "SUPERMAN."
I HEAR YOU'RE LOOKING FOR A NEW STRIP TO REPLACE "ZATARA THE MAGICIAN" IN ACTION COMICS.
TAXI

GOOD! HAVE YOUR PEOPLE CALL MY PEOPLE.
WE'LL DO LUNCH.
End

# SKETCHES

## ADAM HUGHES

There's an odd feeling you get when working with an industry "name" like Stan. He's never seemed "real" to me, a guy who never met him. Actually getting the opportunity to work with someone who's been an integral part of comics since long before I was even born was a daunting task.

Scarier still was being asked to not only produce covers for the series, but to help design Stan Lee's Superman for John Buscema. Doing a design for a character you know is going to be drawn by a legendary artist can really affect your decision-making skills. Since John was to draw Stan's SUPERMAN, I thought making him as tough-looking as I could would be appropriate. Mr. Buscema drew the manliest men in comics; there never was any question if one of his characters picked posies or wrote their insecurities down in journals. Designing characters is *not* my strong suit. My only direction was that Stan's Superman was an alien policeman, and that he didn't *have* to have the trademark colors of the regular Superman. Stan also said that his Supes was supposed to be a real hardcase — sort of a Kryptonian Clint Eastwood.

I tried to give his outfit some elements of a Canadian Mountie, probably the most recognizably archetypal cops in the world: red tunic, epaulets, etc. I just thought if there were some military/law enforcement cuts to his suit, it might make the reader subconsciously think "police." I made his hair short and cropped, as if he didn't give a damn about his appearance, and probably cut it himself. Editor Mike Carlin suggested the "S"-shaped scar running down his face.

All in all, this Superman is *not* a guy you want to perpetrate no-goodness anywhere in the vicinity of.

**— Adam Hughes**

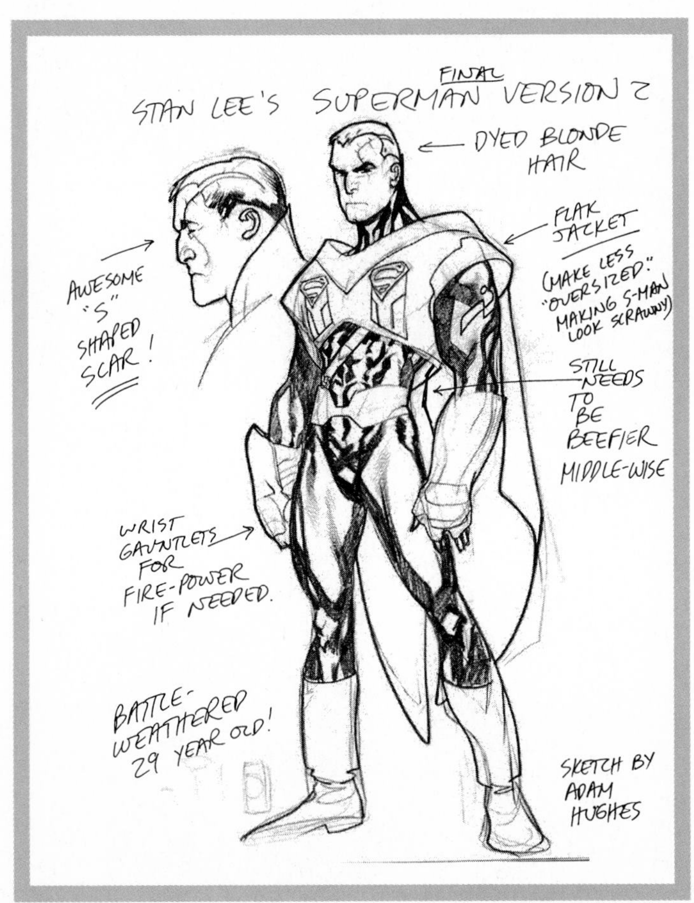

SKETCHES

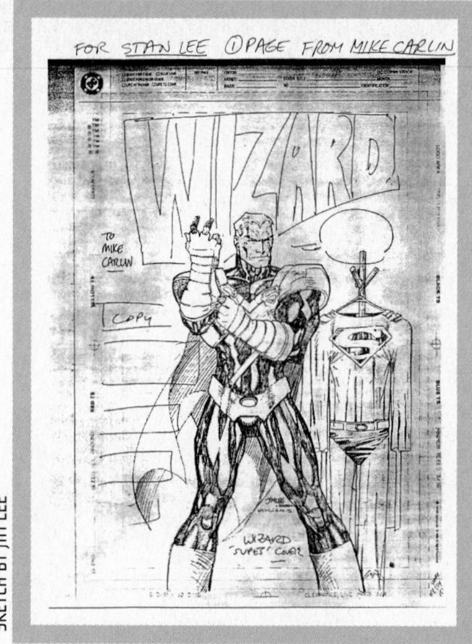


SKETCH BY JIM LEE

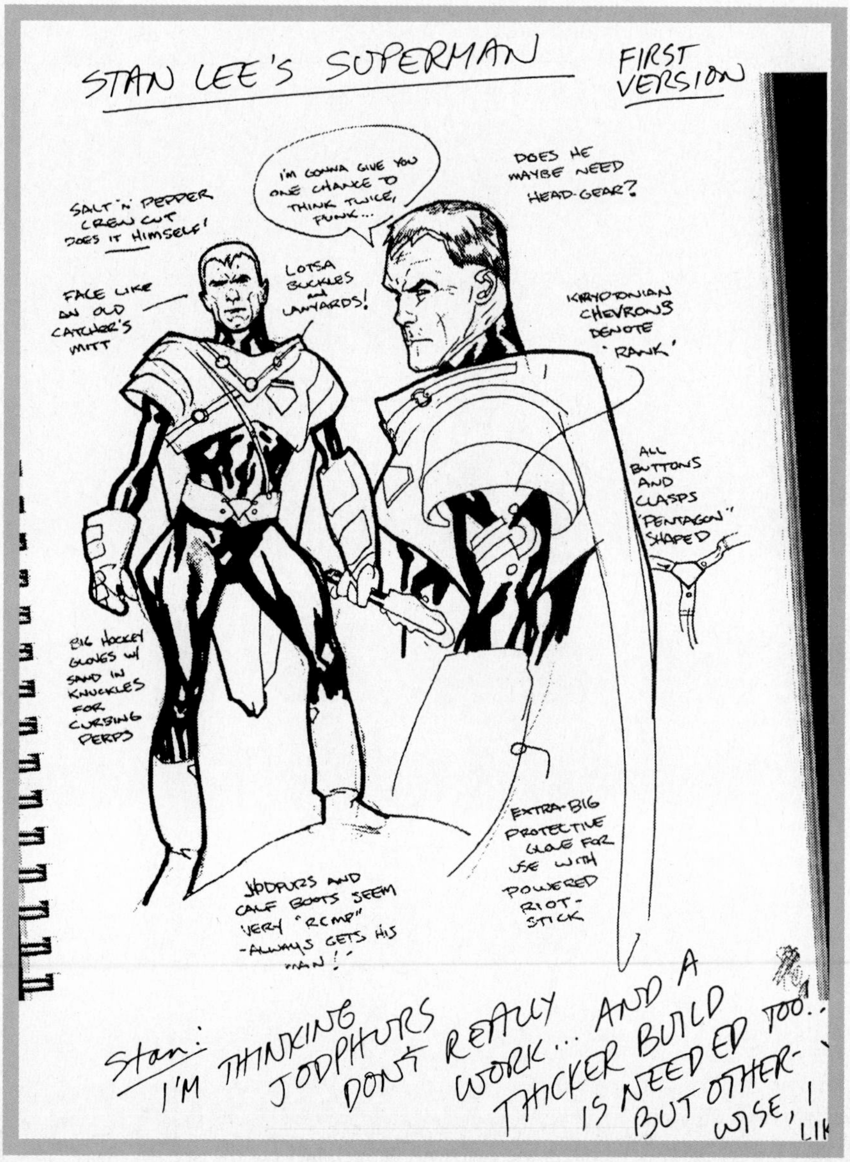

STAN LEE'S SUPERMAN

FIRST VERSION

I'M GONNA GIVE YOU ONE CHANCE TO THINK TWICE, PUNK...

DOES HE MAYBE NEED HEAD-GEAR?

SALT 'N' PEPPER CREW CUT DOES IT HIMSELF!

LOTSA BUCKLES AND LANYARDS!

FACE LIKE AN OLD CATCHER'S MITT

KRYPTONIAN CHEVRONS DENOTE 'RANK'

ALL BUTTONS AND CLASPS "PENTAGON" SHAPED

BIG HOCKEY GLOVES W/ SAND IN KNUCKLES FOR CURBING PERPS

EXTRA-BIG PROTECTIVE GLOVE FOR USE WITH POWERED RIOT-STICK

JODPURS AND CALF BOOTS SEEM VERY "RCMP" - ALWAYS GETS HIS MAN!

Stan: I'M THINKING JODPHURS DON'T REALLY WORK... AND A THICKER BUILD IS NEEDED TOO... BUT OTHER-WISE, I LIK

THE CHURCH OF ETERNAL EMPOWERMENT.
A CHURCH LIKE ANY OTHER CHURCH.
OR SO IT SEEMS.
Church of Eternal Empowerment REVEREND dominic darrk
REV. DOMINIC DARRK ABRUPTLY TURNS FROM HIS CONGREGATION...
EXALTED ONE--?
LEAVE ME!
LET HIM WHO SERVES ME IN A DISTANT LAND APPEAR BEFORE ME, BY MY COMMAND!
CRAGG CROGOR, HAVE YOU FOUND IT YET?
N-NO, EXALTED ONE. WE ARE STILL LOOKING.
I AM SORELY DIS-PLEASED.
I WILL ABIDE NO EXCUSES.
FIND IT, CRAGG CROGOR. --FOR WELL YOU KNOW THE PENALTY FOR FAILURE.
AT A GESTURE FROM DARRK, THE HOLOGRAM VANISHES.
IT MUST BE FOUND.
ONLY I AM DESTINED TO HAVE IT.
AND HAVE IT I SHALL.

LOS ANGELES UNIVERSITY.
A UNIVERSITY LIKE ANY OTHER UNIVERSITY.
NOT TOO UNUSUAL.
BUT WE HAVE TO START SOMEWHERE.
HEY, YOU'RE GOIN' THE WRONG WAY.
CLASSES ARE OVER.
IT'S TIME TO PARTY!
Uh-uh, NO WAY!
PROFESSOR LEWIS IS GIVING A SPECIAL LECTURE.
GET REAL! HE'S ABOUT ARCHAEOLOGY. IT'S, LIKE, DULL CITY!
NOT THE WAY HE TEACHES IT.
YOU ASK WHY I'M INTO ARCHAEOLOGY?
'CAUSE IT'S THE MOST EXCITING SUBJECT I KNOW!
IT'S MORE THAN DIGGING UP OLD BONES...
IT'S ABOUT MAGIC AND LEGENDS, MONSTERS AND MYTHS.
IT GOES BEYOND THE WILDEST STRETCHES OF YOUR IMAGINATION.
LIKE, HOW?

WHAT IF EARTH HAD BEEN VISITED BEFORE?
WHAT IF AN ALIEN RACE TAUGHT THE EGYPTIANS TO BUILD THE PYRAMIDS?
WHAT IF THE SPHINX WAS EGYPT'S TRIBUTE TO THAT RACE?
WAS THERE A COSMIC REASON FOR THE FALL OF ATLANTIS?
WHERE DO LEGENDS COME FROM? WHAT IF THEY'RE ALL BASED ON FACTS?
WHAT IF SOMEONE LIKE ALADDIN REALLY HAD A MAGIC LAMP AGES AGO?
WHAT IF THOSE SAME ALIENS LEFT SUCH A LAMP BEHIND--
--A LAMP WITH STRANGE POWERS?
ALL SUCH LEGENDS MAY HAVE ORIGINATED FROM ONE SOURCE--
FROM A RACE SO ANCIENT THAT ONLY THE TALES REMAIN?
IS HE FOR REAL?
WHAT'S HE BEEN SMOKIN'?
HE KNOWS MORE THAN HE'S TELLING.
I CAN SENSE IT!

A WORK FORCE IN AFRICA.
LED BY CRAGG CROGOR.
A BOSS LIKE ANY OTHER BOSS.
DON'T YOU BELIEVE IT!
MOVE IT, YOU WORTHLESS CRUMBBUMS!
YOU'LL FIND WHAT I'M LOOKIN' FOR, OR YA'LL ANSWER TO ME!
HEY, LOOK, I'M GONNA BAG ME A HIPPO!
WHY? HE WON'T BOTHER US.
DAMN STRAIGHT! NOT AFTER I DRILL 'IM!
THIS IS AN ANIMAL PRESERVE.
YOUR MEN HAVE BROKEN THE LAW!
'ZAT SO?
CAN'T PROVE NOTHIN' WITHOUT WITNESSES.
AND SINCE YOU'RE THE ONLY WITNESSES--!
TOO BAD THEY TRIPPED AN' FELL OFF THE HILL!
YEAH! IT'LL BE A CRYIN' SHAME IF NO ONE FINDS 'EM TILL WE'RE LONG GONE!
AWRIGHT! YA ALL HAD YER FUN. NOW GIT MOVIN'!
WE'LL FIND WHAT WE'RE AFTER BY NIGHTFALL--OR ELSE!

EXCUSE ME, PROFESSOR. I'M CATHY WARREN.
I KNOW. YOU'VE BEEN AT EVERY LECTURE.
YOU MEAN--YOU NOTICED ME?
COULDN'T HELP IT. YOU'RE NOT UNATTRACTIVE.
I-I'M FLATTERED.
UNFORTUNATELY, CATHY, I'M IN A HURRY. I'M CATCHING A PLANE TO AFRICA.
I'M SEEKING THE MOST IMPORTANT ARCHAEOLOGICAL FIND OF ALL--
THE ONE THING THAT UNITES ALL OTHER LEGENDS--
THE FABLED TREE OF LIFE.
TREE of LIFE
BUT ISN'T IT JUST A FAIRY TALE?
--LIKE SEARCHING FOR RUMPLESTILTSKIN?
I HOPE NOT.
THE TREE OF LIFE IS MENTIONED IN EVERY RELIGION.
IT'S AT THE BEGINNING OF GENESIS IN THE BIBLE.
AND THE BOOK OF REVELATION ENDS WITH THE TREE OF LIFE.
I--DIDN'T KNOW.
THE DANES REFER TO IT AS YGGDRASIL.
IT APPEARS IN MAYAN LEGENDS AND IN THE KABALLAH.
ABDU'L-BAHA CALLS IT THE COVENANT BETWEEN GOD AND MAN.
BUT THERE'S MORE--
IT REPRESENTS THE GREATEST SOURCE OF POWER THE WORLD HAS EVER KNOWN.
BUT WHY ARE YOU GOING TO AFRICA?
BECAUSE IT'S THE CRADLE OF MANKIND.
THAT'S WHERE I HOPE TO FIND IT.
I'LL-- I MEAN-- WE'LL MISS YOU.
SOMEONE ELSE SUSPECTS THE TRUTH.
WHAT ARE MY ORDERS?

AND, SPEAKING OF AFRICA...
WHAT'S THE HOLDUP?
WE GO NO FURTHER.
THIS PLACE CURSED!
THINK ABOUT IT, YELLABELLY.
THIS GUN'LL KILL YA FASTER THAN ANY CURSE.
NO! BULLET CAN ONLY KILL.
BUT BEYOND GREEN MIST-- IS WORSE THAN DEATH!
MAYBE WE OUGHTA THINK IT OVER, BOSS.
YEAH, THIS PLACE AIN'T ON ANY MAP.
AIN'T NEVER SEEN GREEN MIST LIKE THAT BEFORE.
SHUDDUP! CRAGG CROGOR DON'T STOP FOR NOTHIN'!
AIN'T NO CRUDDY QUICKSAND GONNA STOP US.
PROBABLY JUST ORDINARY MUD ANYHOW.
OKAY, SO IT'S SINKIN'. NO BIG DEAL.
CAN'T BE ALL THAT DEEP.
LOOK, I'LL PROVE IT TO YA.
BE CAREFUL, BOSS.

I-IT'S LIKE THE BLASTED QUICKSAND PULLED IT OUTTA MY HAND!
LOOK AT IT GO! I AIN'T NEVER FELT SUCH FORCE!
A CRUMMY BOG CAN'T BEAT ME!
ROLL IN THE BULLDOZER!
YEAHHH! THAT'S HOW T'DO IT.
WE'LL TEAR DOWN THE LOUSY TREES AN' MAKE OUR OWN PATH AROUND THE QUICKSAND!
THEY CAN TAKE THEIR CRUMMY CURSE AN' SHOVE IT!
BOSS! LOOKS LIKE A TORNADO STARTED UP IN THERE!
IT'S TEARIN' THE 'DOZER APART!
THIS AIN'T HUMAN. SOME-THIN' SPOOKY'S GOIN' ON.
THE LEGENDS ARE TRUE. THE GODS PROTECT THEIR OWN.
SHUDDUP N' PACK. WE'RE GETTIN' OUTTA HERE.

rtures
AN AIRPORT.
LIKE ANY OTHER AIRPORT.
WE PLAY NO FAVORITES.
SOMEONE CALLING ME?
OH, CATHY.
WHAT A COINCIDENCE. WHERE ARE YOU FLYING TO?
SAME PLACE AS YOU.

CROGOR! LOOK! WHAT'S THAT--UP THERE?
A HOLOGRAM'S FORMING.
MUST BE IMPORTANT--IF HE'S WILLING TO SHOW HIMSELF TO EVERYONE!
CRAGG CROGOR, YOU DISAPPOINT ME.
YOUR MISSION HAS FAILED.
NO, EXALTED ONE! WE'RE STILL SEARCHING!
BUT FEAR AND COWARDICE HAVE DRIVEN YOU FROM THE APPOINTED PLACE.
NO! I JUST FIGGERED THERE AIN'T NOTHIN' THERE...
THEN RETURN YOU TO THE PLACE WHENCE YOU CAME.
FOR THAT WHICH YOU SEEK LIES BEYOND THE GREEN MIST.
AND KNOW YOU THIS, CRAGG CROGOR...
HOWEVER MUCH YOU MAY FEAR THE TERROR OF THE FORBIDDEN SITE...
...IT WILL BE AS NOTHING TO THE TERROR OF--MY WRATH!
AWRIGHT! WHAT'RE YOU STANDIN' AROUND FOR?
WE'RE GOIN' BACK.
WE'RE GONNA BLAST OUR WAY PAST THAT QUICKSAND, NO MATTER WHAT!
AND ANYONE WHO EVEN THINKS OF CUTTIN' OUT--
--WILL BE A DEAD MAN BEFORE HE CAN MAKE A MOVE!

A COINCIDENCE.
JUST LIKE ANY COINCIDENCE.
'CAUSE IT MAKES IT EASIER TO TELL OUR TALE.
BUT WHY WON'T YOU GUIDE US THERE?
IF IT'S A TOUGH TREK WE'LL PAY YOU DOUBLE!
MONEY IS NO GOOD TO THE DEAD.
THERE IS A CURSE UPON THE FORBIDDEN ZONE.
BUT I'VE GOT THIS MAP...
NO! PUT IT AWAY! I WILL NOT LOOK!
GO IF YOU MUST, BUT NOT WITH US!
THE JEEP'S GASSED UP AND WE'RE TRAVELING LIGHT.
WE'LL GET THERE ON OUR OWN.
I WONDER WHAT THEY WERE SO AFRAID OF.
HALF A DAY LATER...
WOW. LOOKS LIKE A TORNADO HIT THE PLACE.
THAT GREEN MIST-- I'VE NEVER SEEN ANYTHING LIKE IT!
COULD BE SOME SORT OF FREAKISH WEATHER CONDITION.
MUST'A BEEN A HELLUVA STORM-- AND SOME OF IT'S STILL RAGING.
SCRATCH THIS FROM MY TOP TEN LIST OF GREAT VACATION SPOTS!
WHAT ARE YOU STARING AT?
I DUNNO. LOOKS LIKE MUD.
BUT WHY THE GREEN GLOW?
NO, IT'S NOT PLAIN MUD. IT CAN'T BE.
CAREFUL. MAYBE YOU SHOULDN'T TOUCH IT.
HAVE TO, OR ELSE I'LL NEVER KNOW.
IT'S MOVING.
LIKE IT'S-- ALIVE-- IN SOME WAY.

LEN, CAN YOU TELL WHAT THE GREEN STUFF IS?
WELL, WELL, LOOK WHAT WE GOT HERE!
ONE THING MISSIN' FROM OUR LITTLE TEAM. A PRETTY LITTLE FILLY.
LEN! BEHIND YOU! LOOK OUT!
HEY, TAKE YOUR GRUBBY HANDS OFF THAT GIRL!
LISTEN UP, GUYS, TO THE BIG, BRAVE HERO!
THAT HERO STUFF MAY WORK IN MOVIES, SONNY--
--BUT THIS IS FOR REAL.
SO SAY GOODBYE TO THE LITTLE LADY.
YOU--YOU KILLED HIM!
NAH, JUS' A LITTLE FLESH WOUND.
A MUD BATH'LL FIX 'IM UP!
YOU TRIGGER-HAPPY FOOL! YOU RUINED EVERYTHING!
HE WAS OUR ONE CHANCE OF FINDING WHAT WE'RE AFTER!
YOU KNOW WHAT DARRK'LL DO IF WE FAIL!
WE AIN'T GONNA FAIL!
WE KNOW IT'S HERE SOMEWHERE!
WE'RE STAYIN' TILL WE FIND IT!

I'VE BEEN-- FATALLY WOUNDED.
I'M SINKING-- THROUGH A THICK, AIRLESS OOZE-- OF GREEN SLIME.
YET--I'M BREATHING --AND THINKING.
I'M ALIVE!
OR--AM I KIDDING MYSELF?
HOW DO I KNOW I'M NOT DEAD?
MAYBE THIS IS WHAT DEATH REALLY IS!
NO, LEONARD LEWIS, THOU DOST LIVE.
FOR REASONS OF MINE OWN, I HAVE POSTPONED THY DEATH.
THINE EARS HEAR NOT MY WORDS.
THEY ARE MEANT FOR THY MIND ALONE.
MEN HAVE CALLED ME YGGDRASIL, THE TREE OF LIFE.
BUT NOW, PAUSE I MUST, FOR THY WOUNDS NEED MINISTER-ING.
THERE! LET TENDRILS AND CREEPERS SPREAD HEALING JUICES UPON THEE.
AND NOW, OPEN THY MIND, FOR THOU SHALT LEARN OF WONDROUS THINGS.

LONG BEFORE THE DAWN OF MAN, OTHERS INHABITED THIS EVER-CHANGING PLANET.
WHENCE THEY CAME NEED NOT CONCERN THEE.
BUT COSMIC DISASTERS BEFELL, CAUSING THEM TO FLEE.
ONLY I, IMMORTAL YGGDRASIL, REMAIN--TO AID AND SHEPHERD THY RACE.
BUT NOW, MAN HIMSELF HATH BECOME HIS OWN GREATEST ENEMY.
MAN HIMSELF DOTH DESTROY THE RAIN-FORESTS, THE WHALES, THE VERY AIR HE BREATHES.
AND IF NOT UNCHECKED, AS SURELY AS NIGHT DOTH FOLLOW DAY, MAN WILL FINALLY DESTROY-- HIMSELF.

BOTH THY BODY AND THY MIND HAVE I PROBED.
I FIND THEE PURE IN SPIRIT AND COURAGEOUS OF HEART.
I POSSESS THE POWER TO GIVE THEE LIFE ANEW.
AND SINCE THOU ART WORTHY--
--DEATH SHALL NOT CLAIM THEE THIS ONE TIME.
ACCEPT YOU NOW THIS LIFE-FORCE WHICH CAN SAVE THEE.
THE LIFE-FORCE I NOW TRANSFER TO THINE OWN MORTAL FORM.
THUS, AFTER COUNTLESS MILLENNIA, I ABANDON THESE GREEN-MISTED ROOTS...
FOR WHERE E'RE THE LIFE-FORCE GOETH, THERE GOETH I.
FROM THIS MOMENT FORTH, MY SPIRIT SHALL RESIDE WITHIN THYSELF.
WHAT E'RE BEFALLS THE HUMAN LEONARD LEWIS--
THOU SHALT FACE IT WITH THE POWER OF--YGGDRASIL.

RISE THEE NOW AND SOAR AT WILL.
THOU ART TRULY FREE AT LAST.
THOU HAST THE HUMAN RACE TO SERVE.
THOU HAST A PLANET TO PROTECT.
MY BODY-- IT GLOWS AND GLEAMS-- LIKE A MYSTICAL GREEN LANTERN!
AND SO SHALT THOU BE KNOWN-- TILL THE END OF THY DAYS.
MY WOUNDS ARE GONE!
I'M MYSELF AGAIN!
EVERYTHING'S BACK TO NORMAL!
AW, C'MON, LEN LEWIS WHO'RE YOU KIDDING?
NOTHING'LL EVER BE NORMAL FOR ME AGAIN!
THE GREEN MIST IS FADING AWAY.
THE QUICK-SAND'S MELTING INTO THE EARTH.
IT'S LIKE THEIR JOB IS OVER, AND THEY KNOW IT!

EVEN YGGDRASIL IS TRANSFORMING, SHRINKING, STARTING TO BLEND WITH THE FOREST ITSELF.
I MUSTN'T THINK ABOUT IT-- NOT NOW--NOT YET-- OR IT COULD DRIVE ME MAD!
CATHY! I'VE GOT TO FIND CATHY.
BUT HOW DO I GET OUT OF HERE?
NO SOONER DOES THAT THOUGHT REGISTER ON LEN LEWIS, THAN...
YGGDRASIL! IT'S GIVEN ME THE POWER OF FLIGHT!
ALL I NEED DO IS THINK OF IT--
--AND I'M TRANSFORMED INTO THE GREEN LANTERN!
AND ONCE I LAND, I CAN THINK MYSELF BACK TO LEN LEWIS AGAIN.
THIS IS WILDER THAN THE LEGENDS I USED TO TEACH.
BUT WHAT DO I DO NOW?
WHERE COULD THOSE KILLERS HAVE TAKEN CATHY?
YOU!
LOOKS LIKE I'LL GET MY ANSWER SOONER THAN I THOUGHT!

YOU WERE TERRIFIC, CATHY.
BUT WHO IS HE? HOW DO YOU KNOW HIM?
IT'S A LONG STORY. THE IMPORTANT THING IS--
--HOW DID YOU SURVIVE THE QUICKSAND?

AND WHAT DID YOU FIND UNDER THERE?
NO TIME FOR THAT NOW.
I'LL TELL YOU WHEN WE'RE IN THE CLEAR.

WHAT'RE WE WAITIN' FOR, CROGOR?
LET'S GO AFTER 'EM!
RELAX, MAN. EVERYTHING'S GOIN' ACCORDIN' TO PLAN.
SHE'S GOTTA FIND OUT EVERY-THING HE KNOWS.
JUST GIVE ME A HINT WHAT WAS UNDER THE QUICKSAND.
NOT NOW. I HEAR THEM COMING AFTER US!
OKAY, I GUESS SHE HAD ENOUGH TIME.

WHY ARE YOU STOPPING?
GOT AN IDEA.
A LITTLE PSYCHOLOGY MIGHT STOP THEM.

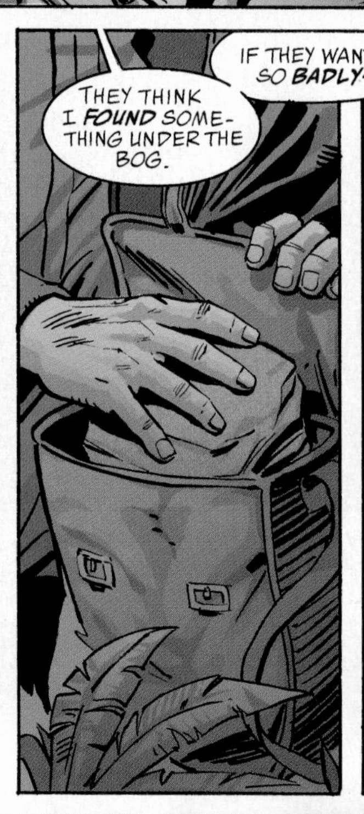
THEY THINK I FOUND SOME-THING UNDER THE BOG.
IF THEY WANT IT SO BADLY--

--I'LL JUST LET THEM HAVE IT!
BUT YOU PUT A WORTHLESS ROCK IN YOUR SHOULDER BAG.
WE KNOW THAT-- BUT THEY DON'T.

HOLD IT. THAT'S JUST WHAT I WANTED!
WHATEVER HE FOUND DOWN THERE--
--HE TOSSED IT SO WE WON'T GET IT.

LET 'EM GO.
THEY DON'T MATTER NO MORE.
WE GOTTA GET WHAT'S IN THAT SACK!

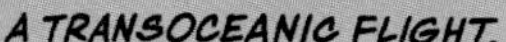
A TRANSOCEANIC FLIGHT.
LIKE ANY OTHER TRANS-OCEANIC FLIGHT.
EXCEPT IT HERALDS THE COMING OF A NEW SUPERHERO.
HAVE YOU HEARD THE NEWS REPORT, LEN?
YES. THE STRANGE GEOLOGICAL UPHEAVALS IN CENTRAL AFRICA HAVE ENDED.
AND THE WEATHER IN THAT REGION IS BACK TO NORMAL.
I WONDER WHAT HAPPENED-- AND WHY.

WHAT FORCE COULD HAVE BEEN POWERFUL ENOUGH TO AFFECT SCIENTIFIC INSTRUMENTS WORLD-WIDE?
I'VE NO IDEA, CATHY.
NOW, AT LAST, YOU CAN TELL ME WHAT YOU FOUND IN THE BOG.

IT WASN'T A THING, MORE LIKE AN EMOTION.
IT AFFECTED ME -- RIGHT HERE.
THAT'S ALL YOU CAN TELL ME?

I DON'T KNOW HOW ELSE TO DESCRIBE IT.
THEN I'VE WASTED A WEEK OF MY LIFE.
WHAT DO YOU MEAN?
WE'VE NOTHING ELSE TO SAY.

CATHY, YOU HAVEN'T SAID A WORD SINCE--
WAIT! WHERE ARE YOU GOING? WHAT'S WRONG?
NOTHING, EXCEPT THAT DIP IN THE BOG MUST HAVE AFFECTED YOUR MIND.
GOODBYE, PROFESSOR LEWIS.

I HAD A FEELING THAT I SHOULDN'T TELL HER THE TRUTH.
APPARENTLY MY INSTINCT WAS RIGHT.

IT WASN'T ME SHE WAS INTERESTED IN.
IT WAS THE SECRET OF THE GREEN-MISTED BOG. BUT WHY?
SOMEHOW, I DON'T FEEL THAT'S THE LAST I'LL SEE OF HER.
TAXI!
TAXI

RKING
VEL 2
HOW I DREAD MAKING THIS CALL.
DID HE SUSPECT ANYTHING?
G
2
I DON'T BELIEVE SO.
BUT HE'S A MADMAN. HE HAS DELUSIONS.
THERE WAS NOTHING I COULD LEARN FROM HIM.
IN SHORT, YOUR MISSION WAS A FAILURE.
EXALTED ONE, IT WASN'T MY FAULT. I DID MY BEST.
BUT THE ARCHAEOLOGIST STILL LIVES.
SURELY YOU KNOW I ABHOR LOOSE ENDS.
ELIMINATE HIM.
DO NOT FAIL ME AGAIN.
MOST REVEREND MASTER, THE CONGREGATION WAITS.
DISMISS THEM.
THERE SHALL BE NO SERMON TODAY.
THE LANTERN IS HERE. I CAN SENSE IT.
I WILL NOT BE THWARTED.
IT MUST BE MINE.

BY THE POWERS THAT BE, BY THE UNSPEAK-ABLE NAME...
BY THE DARKNESS OF NIGHT, BY THE SHADOW AND FLAME...
BRING MY SERVITOR FORTH, FROM WHEREVER HE BE!
KNOW YOU NOW, CROGOR, YOU HAVE DISPLEASED ME.
HOW--DID I--GET HERE?
I ASK THE QUESTIONS.
WHERE IS THE GREEN LANTERN?
I NEVER SAW 'IM. HE DON'T EXIST.
YOU THINK ME A FOOL?
IT IS YOU WHO SHALL CEASE TO EXIST!
NO, EXALTED ONE--

CAN'T--
BREATHE.
LIKE AN INVISIBLE HAND--
CRUSHING ME--
I HAVE BUT ONE WEAK-NESS.
I AM TOO MERCIFUL.
THOUGH YOU ARE UNDESERV-ING-- I SHALL LET YOU LIVE.
BUT I SHALL GOVERN EVERY MOMENT OF YOUR PITIFUL LIFE.
BEHOLD!
WH-WHAT'S HAPPENIN' TO ME?!
THE PAIN WILL BE SHORT-LIVED.
I AM MERELY ALTERING YOUR BODY'S METABOLISM.
A TRIFLING FEAT FOR SUCH AS I.
HENCEFORTH, FOR EACH DAY OF YOUR LIFE--
--YOU SHALL AGE ONE FULL YEAR.
TILL YOU DIE OF OLD AGE WITHIN TWO SHORT MONTHS.
BUT FIND ME THE LANTERN AND I WILL REVERSE THE PROCESS.
NOW GO--WHILE YOU STILL CAN.
ONCE THE POWER OF THE LANTERN IS MINE--
--NOTHING CAN STOP MY COSMIC PLAN!

A PROFESSOR'S BOOK-LINED STUDY.
LIKE ANY ORDINARY PROFESSOR'S STUDY.
BUT THIS IS NO LONGER AN ORDINARY PROFESSOR.
DESPITE ALL THE MIRACULOUS, UNBELIEVABLE THINGS THAT HAVE HAP-PENED--
--I STILL CAN'T GET CATHY OUT OF MY MIND!
THERE WAS SOMETHING ABOUT HER THAT--
OH, THE PHONE!
HEY, I WAS JUST THINKING ABOUT YOU!
MEET YOU? SURE, I'M ON MY WAY!
KANE
SHE SOUNDED NERVOUS... A LITTLE FRANTIC.
I KNOW THERE'S SOMETHING SHE FEARS. IF I COULD JUST-- uh oh.
DON'T HAVE TO BE AN EXPERT TO SPOT A MUGGING IN PROGRESS!
EVEN WITHOUT A SUPER POWER I'D TRY TO HELP.
BUT HERE'S MY CHANCE TO SEE IF THAT GREEN LANTERN THING IS FOR REAL.
I DIDN'T EVEN HAVE TO SAY A MAGIC WORD--
--OR CHANGE IN A PHONE BOOTH.
MAN! ALL IT TAKES IS A THOUGHT!

THIS IS TOO MUCH.
I'M ACTUALLY FLYING!
--JUST AS THOUGH I'VE BEEN DOING IT ALL MY LIFE.

THEY CAN'T BELIEVE WHAT THEY'RE SEEING.
WHY AM I NOT SURPRISED?

AND HOW ABOUT THIS--?
I DON'T EVEN HAVE TO DIRTY MY HANDS ON HIM.
IT'S NOT REAL. IT'S A MOVIE. IT MUST BE.

HE WON'T BE BOTHERING YOU AGAIN.
YOU'VE NOTHING TO WORRY ABOUT.
UNTIL THE MEN IN WHITE COATS TAKE ME AWAY!

I SAW IT! I SAW IT ALL!
I'LL CALL THE PAPERS, THE TV!
I SAW A MIRACLE!

WHAT AN EXPERIENCE. WHAT A RUSH!
IF THIS IS HOW IT FEELS TO BE A SUPERHERO--
--I CAN DEAL WITH IT!
OF COURSE, I'M STILL EXPECTING TO WAKE UP AT ANY MINUTE.
BUT TILL THEN, I MIGHT AS WELL GO WITH THE FLOW.
IT'S HIM! I KNEW HE'D COME TO MEET ME!

THIS IS THE ONLY WAY I CAN SQUARE MYSELF WITH REVEREND DARRK.

THERE MUST BE SOME COSMIC PURPOSE, SOME GRAND DESIGN BEHIND ALL THIS.
MY POWER IS TOO AWESOME TO WASTE ON MUGGERS OR PETTY CROOKS.
NODELL'S
J. Schw
JS
NOW'S MY CHANCE! AS SOON AS I GET CLOSER--
SIRENS! WHERE ARE THEY COMING FROM?

A POLICE CAR-- FOLLOWED BY A NEWS VAN!
WHAT'S GOING ON?
FINGER
POLICE
CAN'T DO IT NOW.
HOW LUCKY CAN HE BE?

WHERE'S THE WOMAN WHO PHONED IN THE REPORT?
HE FLEW. LIKE A BIRD. I SAW HIM.
LATV
I'LL GET ANOTHER CHANCE.

MAN! THE COPS SURE ARRIVED IN RECORD TIME!

AND THERE'S THE PRESS. ANYTHING FOR A STORY.

WITH MY POWER, IT'S NOT HARD TO BE A HERO.

WADDAYA KNOW? HE'S ONE OF OURS.

WHAT HAPPENED, DETECTIVE?

SOME FREAK INTERFERED WITH MY BUST.

HE HELPED THAT DRUG LORD GET AWAY WHO WE'VE BEEN STAKIN' OUT.

YEAH, SOME HERO I AM.

BECAUSE I ACTED WITHOUT THINKING, I HELPED A FELON ESCAPE.

I MUST NEVER FORGET-- POWER MISUSED IS JUSTICE ABUSED.

I SAW HIM! I SAW HIM! HE COULD FLY!

AND GREEN LIGHTNING SHOT OUT OF HIS BODY!

HOO BOY. WHERE'D HE PARK HIS FLYIN' SAUCER?

I KNOW IT SOUNDS CRAZY-- BUT I SAW IT, TOO!

--AND TELL US WHAT YOU SAW, MA'AM.

IT WAS TERRIFYING. LIKE A SCARY HORROR MOVIE.

HE WAS HUGE, DEADLY, A BIG GREEN MONSTER.

NOBODY'S SAFE. WE'RE ALL DOOMED!

LATV NEWS

SONI

IN OTHER NEWS, REV. DOMINIC DARRK IS OFFERING $100,000 FOR INFORMATION ABOUT AN ARTIFACT THAT WAS STOLEN IN AFRICA.

ANYONE HAVING SUCH INFORMATION...

LATV NEWS

SONI

...MAY CONTACT THE CHURCH OF ETERNAL EMPOWER-MENT...

THE POWER OF THE LANTERN IS SO GREAT...

...MEN WILL NEVER STOP SEARCH-ING FOR IT.

LATV NEWS

SONI

THAT MEANS I'VE GOT TO KEEP MY IDENTITY SECRET --ALWAYS.

I HAVE NO PATIENCE FOR WAITING.
THE POWER OF THE GREEN LANTERN MUST BE MINE NOW.
urch of Eternal

INSTEAD OF SEARCHING, LIKE ANY WITLESS SUPPLICANT...
...I'LL MAKE THE GREEN LANTERN COME TO ME.
H-HOW CAN YOU DO THAT, EXALTED ONE?

BY CREATING A GIGANTIC, HORRIFYING MENACE...
SOMETHING SO DESTRUCTIVE THAT, ONCE UN-LEASHED UPON THE CITY...
...NOTHING CAN STOP IT.

THE GREEN LANTERN IS CERTAIN TO TRY TO SAVE LOS ANGELES.
IN SO DOING, HE'LL REVEAL HIMSELF TO ME--
--AND I SHALL CRUSH HIM.
PREPARE YOU NOW TO OPERATE AND CONTROL MY MASTERPIECE OF DESTRUC-TION.
B-BUT IT'LL BE YOUR CREATION. SHOULDN'T YOU CONTROL IT?

HAVE YOU SO SOON FORGOTTEN?
I AM BUT A HUMBLE PREACHER.

A DESERT.
LIKE ANY OTHER CALIFORNIA DESERT.
BUT NOT TODAY.
TODAY IT IS ALSO AN ISOLATED TEST SITE...
...A SITE WHERE A FANTASTIC WORKOUT IS TAKING PLACE.
I'VE GOT TO LEARN THE FULL EXTENT OF MY POWER.
WHAT AM I TRULY CAPABLE OF DOING?
CAN THE GREEN LANTERN PERFORM ANY FEAT IMAGINABLE?
DO I HAVE POWER OVER ALL EARTH'S ELEMENTS?
AM I ABLE TO UNDO WHATEVER IT IS I'VE DONE?
NO. THERE ARE LIMITS. I SEE THAT NOW.
MY POWER IS WEAKENING.
I CAN'T QUITE MOVE THESE BOULDERS BACK TOGETHER.

WHY WAS IT SO EASY WHEN I FIRST STARTED?
WHY IS IT BECOMING MORE DIFFICULT NOW?
I CAN STILL CREATE A WHIRLING SAND STORM.
BUT IT TAKES MORE ENERGY THAN IT DID BEFORE.
AND I STILL HAVE MY MOST AWESOME POWER.
I'M ABLE TO TAKE TO THE SKY.
BUT I'M LOSING ALTITUDE.
I'M DESCENDING-- WITHOUT WILLING MYSELF TO DO SO.
I COULDN'T STAY ALOFT.
COULD JUST BARELY MANAGE TO KEEP FROM LANDING TOO HARD.
I SHOULD HAVE GUESSED. SHOULD HAVE FIGURED IT OUT.
MY POWER'S LIKE A BATTERY.
THE MORE IT'S USED, THE WEAKER IT GETS.
I'LL HAVE TO REST NOW...
...GIVE THE LANTERN TIME TO RECHARGE ITSELF.

DAYS LATER, WE REJOIN A LECTURER.
LIKE ANY OTHER LECTURER.
BUT NOW WITH A STRANGE, INCREDIBLE SECRET.
WELL, I SEE TIME'S UP AGAIN.
BUT I WANT TO LEAVE YOU WITH THIS THOUGHT...
...THERE MIGHT BE MORE TO LEGENDS THAN PEOPLE SUSPECT.
AND THERE'S MORE TO LEONARD LEWIS THAN I SUSPECTED.
THE WAY HE SURVIVED THE GREEN BOG--
--AND THE APPEARANCE OF THE GREEN LANTERN ONCE HE WAS BACK HOME.
BUT I WON'T TRY TO KILL HIM THIS TIME.
I'LL SCORE MORE POINTS BY CAPTURING HIM--
--AND BRINGING HIM TO REV. DARRK AS MY PRISONER.
NO MATTER HOW POWERFUL HE IS...
...I'VE GOT MY GUN.
AND I WON'T BE AFRAID TO USE IT.
HOL
Love Story IV
GARGANTU
SUDDENLY, A STRANGE RUMBLING FILLS THE AIR.
PASSERSBY WONDER--IS IT THEIR IMAGINATION, OR DID THE MONSTROUS BEHEMOTH MOVE?
GARGANTUA
SHOWING SOON!

THE QUESTION ISN'T UNANSWERED FOR LONG.
THE BEHEMOTH MOVED.
AND CONTINUES TO MOVE.
CRUSHING ALL IN ITS PATH.
UA
FIRST COMES SHOCK.
THEN DISBELIEF.
THEN OVER-POWERING AWE.
THEN THE GUT-WRENCHING, MIND-BLASTING, CITY-WIDE TERROR!

WITHIN SECONDS, THE STREETS OF LOS ANGELES TURN INTO BEDLAM.
PEOPLE RUN MINDLESSLY, AIMLESSLY.
WITH ONLY ONE THOUGHT--ESCAPE.
ONE FEMALE HAS ANOTHER OBJECTIVE.
THIS IS MY CHANCE.
DON'T MOVE. DON'T TURN AROUND.
I'VE GOT A GUN.
CATHY.
VERY WELL, I WON'T TURN AROUND.
I'VE SOMETHING MORE IMPORTANT TO DO.
I SUSPECTED IT.
BUT, NOW THAT I'VE SEEN IT--
WAS I MAD?
HOW COULD I HAVE BETRAYED HIM FOR REV. DARRK?
HOW COULD I HAVE TURNED AGAINST--A DEMI-GOD?

I DON'T KNOW WHERE HE CAME FROM-- OR HOW--
--BUT I'VE GOT TO GET HIM AWAY FROM THE BUILD-INGS, FROM THE STREETS.
THIS'LL MAKE HIM NOTICE ME.

GOOD. HE'S TURNING.
IF I CAN JUST LEAD HIM TO A DESERTED AREA--

AW, NO! HE STRUCK THAT ABANDONED BUILDING!
IT'LL CRUSH THE CROWDS BELOW--

--UNLESS MY POWER CAN DISSOLVE IT INTO DUST.
IT WORKED. THEY'RE SAFE.
BUT WHAT ABOUT THE REST OF THE CITY?

HOW CAN I--? DOWN THERE-- THAT'S CATHY.

I'VE GOT TO REACH REV. DARRK.
HAVE TO FIND A WAY TO MAKE HIM STOP SEEKING THE GREEN LANTERN.
OH--MY FOOT--!
CATHY TRIPPED!
SHE'S RIGHT UNDER THE 50-FOOT MONSTER!
DON'T PANIC.
I'LL STOP HIM.
I WONDERED ABOUT THE EXTENT OF MY POWER.
HERE'S WHERE I GET THE ANSWER.
BUT IT'S DOING IT THE HARD WAY.

CAN'T HOLD HIM MUCH LONGER.
ONLY ONE THING TO DO.
HOLD ON TO ME, CATHY.
BEST OFFER I'VE HAD ALL DAY.
IF I CAN GET US AWAY FAST ENOUGH--
YOU DID IT!
THOOM
I HAVE A CONFESSION TO--
NOT NOW. I'VE STILL GOTTA STOP THAT THING.
THAT'S THE MAN I TRIED TO BETRAY.
HOW WILL I EVER BE ABLE TO LIVE WITH MYSELF?

HE'S IN AN OPEN AREA NOW.
SO I CAN GIVE IT ALL I'VE GOT!
I DID IT.
HE'S DOWN!
HE LOOKED REAL. HE SEEMED ALIVE.
BUT HE CAN'T BE.
MY PLAN HAS BORNE FRUIT.
I'VE FOUND THE GREEN LANTERN.
NOW MY BEHEMOTH HAS ONE LAST TASK TO PERFORM.

I'VE GOT TO GO TO HIM... TO APOLOGIZE...
TO BEG HIS FORGIVENESS.
THE MONSTER'S HAND--IT'S MOVING!
IT'S REACHING FOR HIM!
LOOK OUT! IT'S TRYING TO GRAB YOU!
CATHY! GET BACK!
RUN! SAVE YOURSELF!
NOOO! HE'S CRUSHING YOU!
LET HER GO! LET HER GO!!

HE'S FINISHED, CATHY. YOU'LL BE SAFE NOW.
CATHY?
YOU--WERE THE BEST THING-- EVER HAPPENED-- TO ME.
I'M--SO SORRY...
WITH ALL MY POWER--
--I COULDN'T SAVE HER.
THAT'S HIM--THE ONE WHO STOPPED THE MONSTER.
VIEWERS, WE'RE FIRST ON THE SCENE WITH EXCLUSIVE COVERAGE OF THE GREEN LANTERN.
PLEASE TURN AND FACE THE CAMERA.
PLEASE GET OUT OF MY SPACE.
LATV
THE MONSTER WAS MECHANICAL.
BUT WHO CREATED IT-- AND WHY?
YOU DON'T UNDERSTAND --THIS IS LIVE TELEVISION!
SORRY, I'VE NO ROOM ON MY SHELF FOR AN EMMY.

THE LANTERN'S GLOW IS LEADING ME TO THAT BUILDING.
THERE MUST BE A REASON.
THE BIG APE'S FINISHED, CROGOR.
YEAH, PACK UP. WE'RE GETTIN' OUTTA HERE.
NOT YET, MISTER.
I CAN SEE THAT YOU'RE THE ONES WHO CONTROLLED THE MONSTER.
IT'S THE GREEN LANTERN! GET 'IM!
WITH MY POWER, FIGHTIN' A FEW THUGS'LL BE EASY AS--
NO! I'M GETTING WEAKER!
THE "BATTERY'S" RUN DOWN!
GREEN LANTERN, huh? BIG DEAL. HE WUZN'T SO TOUGH!
LUCKILY, THEY CAN'T RECOGNIZE ME AS LEN LEWIS.
THE REVEREND'LL BE MIGHTY GLAD TO SEE 'IM, RIGHT, CROGOR?
YEAH, BUT I GOT ME ANOTHER IDEA.

WE BEEN LIVIN' IN FEAR OF DARRK FOR YEARS, RIGHT?
DAMN STRAIGHT.
WELL, HERE'S OUR CHANCE TO GIT OUT FROM UNDER.
WE MAKE GREEN LANTERN GIVE US THE SECRET OF HIS POWER...
...AN' WE USE IT TO TAKE OVER FROM DARRK.
SO WADDAYA SAY, BALDY? DO YA CATCH A BULLET--
--OR SHOW US HOW YA DO THAT STUFF YOU DO?
YOU DON'T LEAVE ME MUCH CHOICE.
REMEMBER, TRY ANY TRICKS AN' WE SNUFF OUT YER LANTERN.
THAT'S IT. THE LONGER YOU DRIVE, THE MORE MY POWER RECHARGES!
NO WAY I CAN TRICK YOU. JUST DRIVE A LITTLE FURTHER AND YOU'LL SEE HOW I DO WHAT I DO.
WE BEEN DRIVIN' FOR HOURS.
YOU'RE RIGHT. THAT'S LONG ENOUGH. YOU CAN STOP NOW.
BUT THERE'S NOTHIN' HERE.
AIN'T NO REASON T'STOP.
YES, THERE IS. I'VE GOT MY POWER BACK.
DON'T LET HIM GET AWAY!
HOW DO WE STOP 'IM?

YOU WANTED TO LEARN ABOUT MY POWER...
HERE'S YOUR FIRST LESSON.
HE'S BULLET-PROOF!
THEN--WADDA WE GONNA DO?

YOU'RE THROUGH DOING.
NOW IT'S MY TURN--

--TO SHOW YOU THE POWER OF THE GREEN LANTERN!

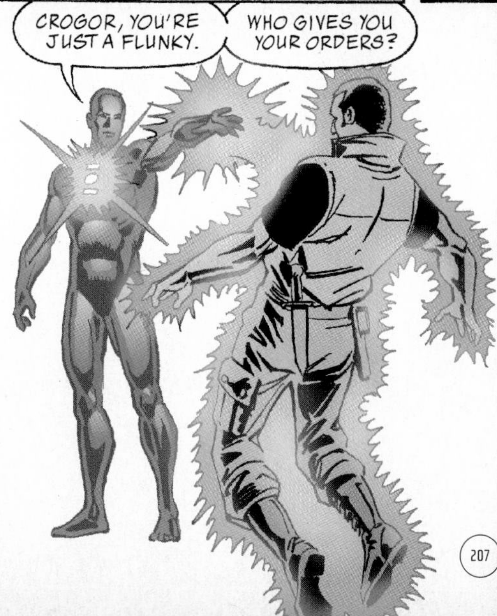
CROGOR, YOU'RE JUST A FLUNKY.
WHO GIVES YOU YOUR ORDERS?

AW, NO! HE'S AGING RAPIDLY--IN FRONT OF MY EYES!
CAN'T--TALK. TOO WEAK--TIRED...

CRAGG CROGOR, I NEED YOUR SERVICES NO LONGER.
TELL ME, MAN-- WHILE YOU CAN!
C-CAN'T BREATHE... MY HEART-- I--I--
HE'S GONE.
HE AGED SIXTY YEARS IN A MATTER OF SECONDS.
YOU, WHO HAVE USURPED THE GIFT THAT SHOULD BE MINE!
YOUR FATE SHALL BE FAR WORSE THAN HIS!
IN A FEW SHORT HOURS, I'VE SEEN THINGS TO MAKE ME QUESTION MY SANITY.
BUT EVERYTHING HAPPENS FOR A REASON.
THERE MUST BE A REASON I WAS GIVEN THIS STRANGE AND AWESOME POWER.
AND AS LONG AS I LIVE, MAY I PROVE TO BE WORTHY OF IT.
END

ON THE STREET
YOU SURE HE'S ONE OF OURS?
WHEN THEY GET SO DEEP UNDER-COVER, NOBODY KNOWS FOR SURE 'CEPT THE TOP-LEVEL FEDS.
IF HE IS KEVIN KING, THE GUY'S A LEGEND!
BIG "IF". COULD BE AN IMPERSONATION.
YOU LOOK LIKE DEATH WARMED OVER.
DUNNO WHAT HIT ME.
NO FEVER. PULSE IS PRETTY WILD, THOUGH.
RUMOR IS KEVIN KING WAS GUNNED DOWN IN A BUST.
YOU GOT MY I.D., MAN.
WELL, DOESN'T MUCH MATTER ANYWAY.
WHAT'S THAT SUPPOSED TO MEAN?

SEEMS WE GOT US SOME REAL-LIFE *COMIC-BOOK HEROES* IN L.A.!

SO WHAT?
SO WHAT GOOD ARE NORMAL COPS ANYMORE? WE'RE JUST *DINOSAURS!*
POLICE
LOS ANGELES
1101
THAT'S A CROCK! NO MASK OR COSTUME CAN REPLACE THIS BADGE!

THAT WAS TRUE *YESTERDAY*, KING. EVERYTHING'S CHANGED *TODAY.*

YOU'RE A CYNIC.
BETTER A CYNIC THAN A FOOL.
AND WHERE DO YOU THINK *YOU'RE* GOING?

TO CATCH ME A CERTAIN DRUG DEALER.
132
GET REAL! LET THAT "GREEN LANTERN" DO IT. YOU *CAN'T* COMPETE WITH *HIM!*

AFTER ALL THESE LONG MONTHS OF INVESTIGATION, FOLLOWING LEADS, POUNDING THE STREETS...
NO WAY I'M GIVING UP THIS CASE.
SPEEDY'S
EVENIN', LOUIE.
YOU KNOW THE ROUTINE: I ASK WHERE I CAN FIND YOUR BOSS... YOU CLAIM YOU KNOW NUTHIN'... AND I SMASH YOUR--
KING! CHILL OUT, MAN! I'LL TELL YA EVERYTHING I KNOW.

DON'T SMART LIP, MAN! YOU THINK I'M STUPID? YOU'VE NEVER SPILLED YOUR GUTS BEFORE!
THAT WAS THEN. THIS IS NOW. THINGS HAVE CHANGED.

MY SCAMS WERE ALWAYS LOW RISK/HIGH RETURN. NOT NOW WITH SUPER-HEROES FLYIN' ALL OVER L.A.
I'M ON YOUR SIDE NOW.

YOUR MAN'S AT 999 DURRELL STREET.
THE BLIMP LOOKS LIKE HE MEANS IT.
GLAD I COULD HELP.
ABBY'S BAR

YESTERDAY IT WOULDA BEEN CONSIDERED EARTHQUAKE DAMAGE-- TODAY IT'S JUST THE TYPICAL RESULT OF A SUPER-POWERED BATTLE.
CRIMINALS SUDDENLY RETIRING 'CAUSE SOME SUPER-TYPES SHOW? THIS IS LIKE TOO EASY.
HOLLY
GARGAN
IF THOSE COSTUMED CLOWNS CAN SPOOK THE BADDIES INTO GIVING UP, THEN WHO NEEDS GUYS LIKE ME?
LOOTER!
FREEZE! POLICE!
WHAT PART OF "FREEZE" DON'T YOU UNDERSTAND?
JUST STAY PUT 'TIL MY BACKUP ARRIVES! CAPISCE?
NO PROBLEMO. BETTER YOU THAN ONE OF THEM SUPER-CHARGED FREAKS!

WITHIN MINUTES...
LOOTER. BOOK HIM.
C'MON, JAIL ME BEFORE THAT GREEN GUY TURNS ME IN-SIDE OUT OR SOME-THIN'!
POLICE
GOTTA STAY FOCUSED... DURRELL STREET...
...I MAY NOT BE SUPER, BUT I GOT A JOB TO DO!
A FIRE!
GAS LINE MUST'VE RUPTURED WHEN THE GREEN DUDE AND THE RED WHATCHACALLIT MIXED IT UP!
AWWW... NO! THERE'S A KID TRAPPED IN THERE!
ANYONE CALLED THE FIRE DEPART-MENT?
WHAT FOR? SOME SUPER-JOE'LL COME ALONG AND SAVE HER.
THE SUPER-HEROES CAN'T BE EVERY-WHERE!
THAT GIRL'S IN DANGER!
THERE SHE IS.
COUGH! COUGH!
DON'T BE SCARED, HONEY!
WE'LL MAKE IT OUT OF HERE.

L.A. PRECINCT 704...

NOW WHAT'S HAPPENING?

WHAT'S GOING ON?

WE'RE HERE TO JOIN UP!

WE WANNA BE COPS!

ALL OF YOU? ALL OF A SUDDEN?

YEAH, MAN, YEAH--WE SAW WHAT YOU DID!

YOU PROVED IT DON'T TAKE SUPER-POWERS TO BE A HERO.

WE WANNA BE LIKE YOU!

YOU'RE A COP. THINK WE HAVE A CHANCE?

SON... THE WORLD MIGHT HAVE A CHANCE NOW...

...UNLIKE THE DINOSAURS!

END

As a lifelong fanboy, I'd always itched for the chance to work with Stan. He visited England on a promotional tour in the early nineties and we talked then about doing something together. I also found out, at the same time, that a postcard I'd received and treasured way-back-when, in response to a fan letter for *Daredevil* #1, wasn't actually signed by Stan but by (Fabulous) Flo Steinberg!

For a while Stan and I kicked around a Captain America idea, but it got mired down at Marvel Comics editorial and I sadly resigned myself to having missed the opportunity.

Then, out of the blue, eight years later, I got a call from Mike Carlin asking me if I'd like to work with Stan on, of all things, Green Lantern! It took me about half a nanosecond to say yes.

Working with Stan was all I had hoped. Starting with his first draft as a foundation, he warmly welcomed my contributions and suggestions. Two things struck me: first, the strength of the original story's structure and the highly effective intercutting of scenes. Secondly, the rigorous way in which he discussed my input with me, always relating it to the needs of the story. It was an educative experience for me and renewed my professional appreciation of Stan's storytelling talents and experience.

And the lifelong fanboy in me had an experience far more gosh-wow than getting a mere signed postcard!

**— Dave Gibbons**

# GALLERY

## secret files

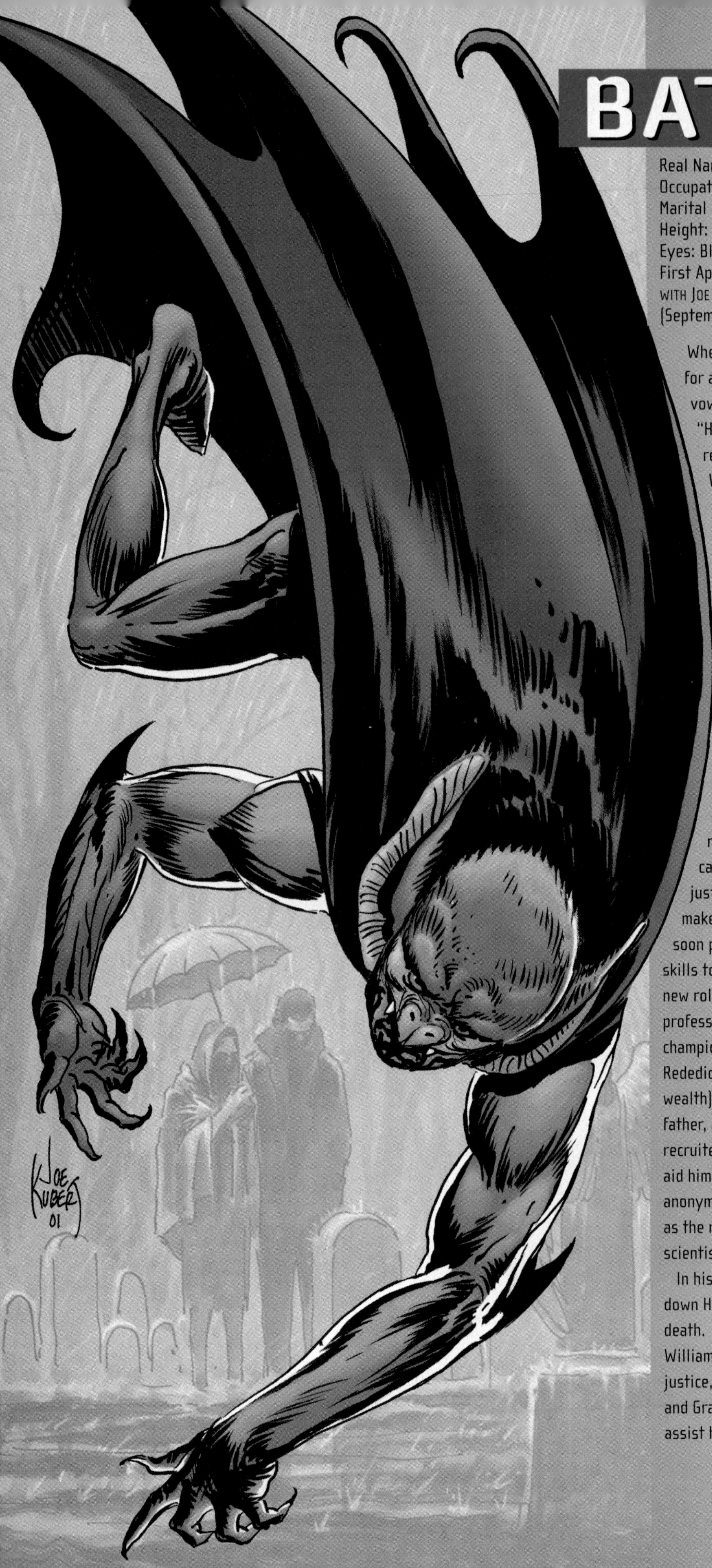


# BATMAN

Real Name: Wayne Williams
Occupation: Professional Wrestler
Marital Status: Single
Height: 6' 3" Weight: 230 lbs.
Eyes: Black Hair: None
First Appearance: JUST IMAGINE STAN LEE WITH JOE KUBERT CREATING BATMAN (September, 2001)

When Wayne Williams was framed for a crime he didn't commit, he vowed revenge on gang leader "Handz" Horgun — the man responsible for sending him to jail. While in prison, he befriended Frederick Grant, a scientist who encouraged Williams to develop his mind and body to their fullest potential. Motivated by Grant and spurred by his desire for vengeance, Williams devoted all his efforts to improving his mind and body while incarcerated, his only company a stray bat.

After stopping a prison riot and saving the Warden's life, Williams was granted early release and immediately began carrying out his plans to exact justice on those who framed him. To make the money his plans required, he soon put his muscular build and mental skills to work, making a fortune in his new role as the world's most famous professional wrestler: the masked champion known only as Batman. Rededicating his life (and his new wealth) to helping people, as his late father, a police officer, once did, Williams recruited the recently released Grant to aid him in his crusade. To preserve his anonymity, Williams allows Grant to act as the millionaire, while he poses as the scientist's bodyguard.

In his first adventure, Batman tracked down Handz, who accidentally fell to his death. No longer seeking vengeance, Williams still continues his mission of justice, with only his intellect, strength and Grant's scientific wizardry to assist him.

# WONDER WOMAN

Real Name: Maria Mendoza
Occupation: Editor's Assistant, *The National Exposer*
Marital Status: Single
Height: 5' 8"  Weight: 115 lbs.
Eyes: Brown  Hair: Black
First Appearance: Just Imagine Stan Lee with Jim Lee Creating Wonder Woman (October, 2001)

Maria Mendoza was a beautiful young idealist who longed for the days when her Peruvian homeland was untouched and full of life. But because of the rich and evil Armando Guitez, the sacred lands she cherished were ruined. Guitez had been searching for Incan runes that would bestow incredible powers on whoever found them, a search Mendoza's father — a local judge — allowed to proceed at great cost to the area's historic shrines.

Eventually Maria's father stood against Guitez and paid for his protest with his life, killed by Guitez in front of an outraged Maria, who managed to escape with the help of archaeologist Steve Trevor. Trevor was attempting to protect the ancient runes from Guitez's corrupt grasp, but to no avail. Guitez found the pair and, after shooting Trevor, broke open the runes and was transformed into a frightening and powerful creature created from pure evil. During the chaos that ensued, a mysterious voice — the spirit of The Sun Goddess, protector of the Earth — called out to Maria, leading her to a golden staff. The Sun Goddess's staff transformed Maria into the new protector of the Earth... Wonder Woman. Using her new powers of flight, energy manipulation, and more, she followed the altered Guitez to Los Angeles, defeating him before he could attack mankind. Needing to stay involved in Earth's defense, Maria — Earth's most powerful super-heroine — chose to stay in L.A., keeping tabs on world affairs from the offices of *The National Exposer.*

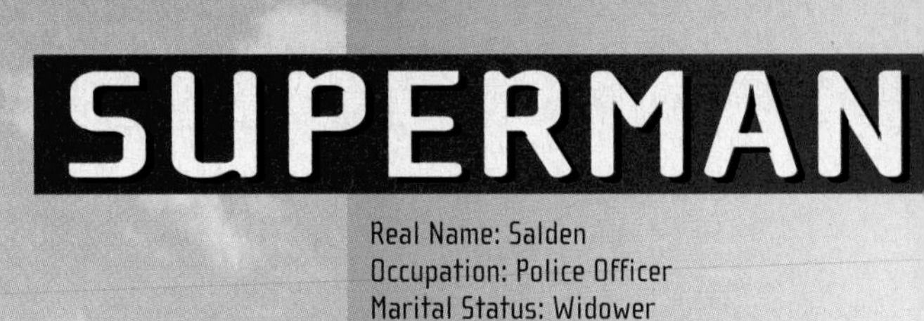

# SUPERMAN

Real Name: Salden
Occupation: Police Officer
Marital Status: Widower
Height: 6' 3" Weight: 240 lbs.
Eyes: Blue Hair: Blond
First Appearance: JUST IMAGINE STAN LEE WITH JOHN BUSCEMA CREATING SUPERMAN (November, 2001)

On a planet in a far-distant galaxy, the Law-Bringer named Salden was the rarest kind of hero. Despite a strenuous exercise regimen, Salden was nowhere near as strong as his fellow officers, who, unlike him, were genetically engineered. But what he lacked in size, he more than made up for in skill... and raw courage.

When Salden's wife, Lyella, was brutally murdered by the villainous Gorrok, Salden chased the killer down, following him onto a prototype spacecraft (one powered by a mysterious green element) just before launch. Gorrok's and Salden's fight caused the ship to go hopelessly out of control, crash-landing into Earth's Pacific Ocean. As Salden swam out of the wreckage, he was unaware that the green element was spreading through the water, giving him the power and strength he always strove for.

Stronger and swifter than everyone else on the planet, Salden was dismayed to learn that Earth was too scientifically backward to return him to his homeworld. Theorizing that Earth's problems dealing with crime and war were responsible for Earth's sluggish scientific evolution, he decided to dedicate his great power to eliminating those distractions.

Needing money to survive, Salden took a job as a circus performer called "Superman." His fantastic skills quickly garnered the attention of many, including entertainment agent Lois Lane (who made him a celebrity overnight). Around the same time, Gorrok was recruited by the mysterious Reverend Dominic Darrk to instigate a war between the United States and China... a plot Salden foiled, besting his hated foe in the process. His enemy defeated, Superman has now turned his attentions squarely on returning home.

Real Name: Len Lewis
Occupation: Professor
Marital Status: Single
Height: 6' 0"   Weight: 190 lbs.
Eyes: Blue   Hair: Blond
First Appearance: JUST IMAGINE STAN LEE WITH DAVE GIBBONS CREATING GREEN LANTERN (December, 2001)

Always in search of a new adventure, archaeology Professor Len Lewis was always in search of new adventures, each one more exciting than the one before. But he never anticipated what was in store for him when he and attractive student Cathy Warren went to Africa in search of Yggdrasil, the legendary Tree of Life, the greatest source of power man has ever known.

Double-crossed by Cathy and shot by Reverend Dominic Darrk's acolytes when he finally located the Tree, all seemed lost... until Len was imbued with the power of the Tree of Life — a power expressed as a green mist pervading the African bog. Transformed into a being 50% human and 50% the energy of Mother Earth, Len was reborn as "Green Lantern," taking his name from the lantern-shaped symbol on his chest.

Created by the Tree of Life to achieve a balance between the needs of nature and the needs of humanity, Green Lantern is a living, glowing vessel harboring each aspect's power in equal measure, forming one complete warrior/defender of both. After mastering his powers, Green Lantern learned that it would be his duty to gather Earth's warriors into a "Justice League," battling the forces of Reverend Darrk and preparing humanity for the Crisis that is to come.

# GREEN LANTERN

# REVEREND DOMINIC DARRK

Real Name: Dominic Darrk
Occupation: Reverend
Marital Status: Married
Height: 6' 4"   Weight: 230 lbs.
Eyes: Purple   Hair: Unknown
First Appearance: JUST IMAGINE STAN LEE WITH JOHN BUSCEMA CREATING BATMAN (Sepember, 2001)

The Reverend Dominic Darrk is the mysterious and charismatic leader of the Church of Eternal Empowerment, which draws followers from all walks of life, courtesy of Darrk recruitment techniques ranging from simple cons to mind control. Though early indications were that Darrk was the ultimate evil on Earth, more recent evidence suggests that there is another power source beyond him. All machinations — whether Darrk's or this mysterious other entity's — are dedicated to overriding the Green Mist generated by Earth's Tree of Life and supplanting it with the purple energy Darrk has wielded in the past.

Darrk and his Church had been paving the way for this unknown force's arrival on Earth for years, with the Church's collective unconsciousness planned to serve as a beachhead for an invasion of both the real world and the Dreamworld. However, the debut of heroes such as Superman, Batman, Wonder Woman, Green Lantern, and the Flash — all in some way created or recruited by Mother Earth — disrupted Darrk's plans. Darrk has spent recent months evaluating Earth's new defenders and has set forces in motion to destroy them. Some of these forces remain hidden, working covertly, while others, acolytes transformed into purple-energy-powered monsters, are more obvious. Once their task is accomplished, Darrk will at last be able to clear the mystic path for the Crisis that is to come and turn Earth and life itself into a living nightmare.

# THE STARS OF THE DC UNIVERSE CAN ALSO BE FOUND IN THESE BOOKS:

## GRAPHIC NOVELS

**ENEMY ACE: WAR IDYLL**
George Pratt

**THE FLASH: LIFE STORY OF THE FLASH**
M. Waid/B. Augustyn/G. Kane/
J. Staton/T. Palmer

**GREEN LANTERN: FEAR ITSELF**
Ron Marz/Brad Parker

**THE POWER OF SHAZAM!**
Jerry Ordway

**WONDER WOMAN: AMAZONIA**
William Messner-Loebs/
Phil Winslade

## COLLECTIONS

**THE GREATEST 1950s STORIES EVER TOLD**
Various writers and artists

**THE GREATEST TEAM-UP STORIES EVER TOLD**
Various writers and artists

**AQUAMAN: TIME AND TIDE**
Peter David/Kirk Jarvinen/
Brad Vancata

**DC ONE MILLION**
Various writers and artists

**THE FINAL NIGHT**
K. Kesel/S. Immonen/
J. Marzan/various

**THE FLASH: BORN TO RUN**
M. Waid/T. Peyer/G. LaRocque/
H. Ramos/various

**GREEN LANTERN: A NEW DAWN**
R. Marz/D. Banks/R. Tanghal/
various

**GREEN LANTERN: BAPTISM OF FIRE**
Ron Marz/Darryl Banks/
various

**GREEN LANTERN: EMERALD KNIGHTS**
Ron Marz/Darryl Banks/
various

**HAWK & DOVE**
Karl and Barbara Kesel/
Rob Liefeld

**HITMAN**
Garth Ennis/John McCrea

**HITMAN: LOCAL HEROES**
G. Ennis/J. McCrea/
C. Ezquerra/S. Pugh

**HITMAN: TEN THOUSAND BULLETS**
Garth Ennis/John McCrea

**IMPULSE: RECKLESS YOUTH**
Mark Waid/various

**JACK KIRBY'S FOREVER PEOPLE**
Jack Kirby/various

**JACK KIRBY'S NEW GODS**
Jack Kirby/various

**JACK KIRBY'S MISTER MIRACLE**
Jack Kirby/various

**JUSTICE LEAGUE: A NEW BEGINNING**
K. Giffen/J.M. DeMatteis/
K. Maguire/various

**JUSTICE LEAGUE: A MIDSUMMER'S NIGHTMARE**
M. Waid/F. Nicieza/J. Johnson/
D. Robertson/various

**JLA: AMERICAN DREAMS**
G. Morrison/H. Porter/J. Dell/
various

**JLA: JUSTICE FOR ALL**
G. Morrison/M. Waid/H. Porter/
J. Dell/various

**JUSTICE LEAGUE OF AMERICA: THE NAIL**
Alan Davis/Mark Farmer

**JLA: NEW WORLD ORDER**
Grant Morrison/
Howard Porter/John Dell

**JLA: ROCK OF AGES**
G. Morrison/H. Porter/J. Dell/
various

**JLA: STRENGTH IN NUMBERS**
G. Morrison/M. Waid/H. Porter/
J. Dell/various

**JLA: WORLD WITHOUT GROWN-UPS**
T. Dezago/T. Nauck/H. Ramos/
M. McKone/various

**JLA/TITANS: THE TECHNIS IMPERATIVE**
D. Grayson/P. Jimenez/
P. Pelletier/various

**JLA: YEAR ONE**
M. Waid/B. Augustyn/
B. Kitson/various

**KINGDOM COME**
Mark Waid/Alex Ross

**LEGENDS: THE COLLECTED EDITION**
J. Ostrander/L. Wein/J. Byrne/
K. Kesel

**LOBO'S GREATEST HITS**
Various writers and artists

**LOBO: THE LAST CZARNIAN**
Keith Giffen/Alan Grant/
Simon Bisley

**LOBO'S BACK'S BACK**
K. Giffen/A. Grant/S. Bisley/
C. Alamy

**MANHUNTER: THE SPECIAL EDITION**
Archie Goodwin/Walter Simonson

**THE RAY: IN A BLAZE OF POWER**
Jack C. Harris/Joe Quesada/
Art Nichols

**THE SPECTRE: CRIMES AND PUNISHMENTS**
John Ostrander/Tom Mandrake

**STARMAN: SINS OF THE FATHER**
James Robinson/Tony Harris/
Wade von Grawbadger

**STARMAN: NIGHT AND DAY**
James Robinson/Tony Harris/
Wade von Grawbadger

**STARMAN: TIMES PAST**
J. Robinson/O. Jimenez/
L. Weeks/various

**STARMAN: A WICKED INCLINATION...**
J. Robinson/T. Harris/
W. von Grawbadger/various

**UNDERWORLD UNLEASHED**
M. Waid/H. Porter/
P. Jimenez/various

**WONDER WOMAN: THE CONTEST**
William Messner-Loebs/
Mike Deodato, Jr.

**WONDER WOMAN: SECOND GENESIS**
John Byrne

**WONDER WOMAN: LIFELINES**
John Byrne

**DC/MARVEL: CROSSOVER CLASSICS II**
Various writers and artists

**DC VERSUS MARVEL/ MARVEL VERSUS DC**
R. Marz/P. David/D. Jurgens/
C. Castellini/various

**THE AMALGAM AGE OF COMICS: THE DC COMICS COLLECTION**
Various writers and artists

**RETURN TO THE AMALGAM AGE OF COMICS: THE DC COMICS COLLECTION**
Various writers and artists

## OTHER COLLECTIONS OF INTEREST

**CAMELOT 3000**
Mike W. Barr/Brian Bolland/
various

**RONIN**
Frank Miller

**WATCHMEN**
Alan Moore/Dave Gibbons

## ARCHIVE EDITIONS

**THE FLASH ARCHIVES Volume 1**
(FLASH COMICS 104, SHOWCASE 4, 8, 13, 14, THE FLASH 105-108)
J. Broome/C. Infantino/J. Giella/
various

**THE FLASH ARCHIVES Volume 2**
(THE FLASH 109-116)
J.Broome/C. Infantino/J. Giella/
various

**GREEN LANTERN ARCHIVES Volume 1**
(SHOWCASE 22-23, GREEN LANTERN 1-5)

**GREEN LANTERN ARCHIVES Volume 2**
(GREEN LANTERN 6-13)
All by J. Broome/G. Kane/
J. Giella/various

**SHAZAM ARCHIVES Volume 1**
(WHIZ COMICS 2-15)

**SHAZAM ARCHIVES Volume 2**
(SPECIAL EDITION COMICS 1, CAPTAIN MARVEL ADVENTURES 1, WHIZ COMICS 15-20)
All by B. Parker/C.C. Beck/
J. Simon/J. Kirby/various

**THE NEW TEEN TITANS Volume 1**
(DC COMICS PRESENTS 26, THE NEW TITANS 1-8)
Marv Wolfman/George Pérez/
various